George Eliot's
SILAS MARNER

A CONTEMPORARY
LITERARY VIEWS BOOK

Edited and with an Introduction by
HAROLD BLOOM

Printed and bound in the United States of America.

First Printing
1 3 5 7 9 8 6 4 2

Cover illustration: Photofest

Library of Congress Cataloging-in-Publication Data

George Eliot's Silas Marner / edited and with an introduction by Harold Bloom.
p.   cm. — (Bloom's Notes)
Includes bibliographical references (p.) and index.
Summary: Includes a brief biography of the author, thematic and structural analysis of the work, critical views, and an index of themes and ideas.
ISBN 0-7910-4074-7.
1. Eliot, George, 1819–1880. Silas Marner. [1. Eliot, George, 1819–1880. Silas Marner. 2. English literature—History and criticism.] I. Bloom, Harold. II. Series.
PR4670.G46 1995
823'.8—dc20
95-43491
CIP
AC

Chelsea House Publishers
1974 Sproul Road, Suite 400
P.O. Box 914
Broomall, PA 19008-0914

Contents

User's Guide

This volume is designed to present biographical, critical, and bibliographical information on George Eliot and *Silas Marner*. Following Harold Bloom's introduction, there appears a detailed biography of the author, discussing the major events in her life and her important literary works. Then follows a thematic and structural analysis of the work, in which significant themes, patterns, and motifs are traced. An annotated list of characters supplies brief information on the chief characters in the work.

A selection of critical extracts, derived from previously published material by leading critics, then follows. The extracts consist of such things as statements by the author on her work, early reviews of the work, and later evaluations down to the present day. The items are arranged chronologically by date of first publication. A bibliography of Eliot's writings (including a complete listing of books she wrote, cowrote, edited, or translated, along with important posthumous publications), a list of additional books and articles on her and on *Silas Marner*, and an index of themes and ideas conclude the volume.

Harold Bloom is Sterling Professor of the Humanities at Yale University and Henry W. and Albert A. Berg Professor of English at the New York University Graduate School. He is the author of twenty books and the editor of more than thirty anthologies of literature and literary criticism.

Professor Bloom's works include *Shelley's Mythmaking* (1959), *The Visionary Company* (1961), *Blake's Apocalypse* (1963), *Yeats* (1970), *A Map of Misreading* (1975), *Kabbalah and Criticism* (1975), and *Agon: Towards a Theory of Revisionism* (1982). *The Anxiety of Influence* (1973) sets forth Professor Bloom's provocative theory of the literary relationships between the great writers and their predecessors. His most recent books are *The American Religion* (1992) and *The Western Canon* (1994).

Professor Bloom earned his Ph.D. from Yale University in 1955 and has served on the Yale faculty since then. He is a 1985 MacArthur Foundation Award recipient and served as the Charles Eliot Norton Professor of Poetry at Harvard University in 1987–88. He is currently the editor of the Chelsea House series Major Literary Characters and Modern Critical Views, and other Chelsea House series in literary criticism.

Introduction

HAROLD BLOOM

Silas Marner: The Weaver of Raveloe remains a beautiful and highly readable book, still immensely popular 130 years after its initial publication. It is not quite of the aesthetic eminence of George Eliot's masterwork, *Middlemarch,* but only because it is much the less ambitious novel, far shorter and confined as it is to a small village in the Midlands. Its protagonists are simple people, seen against a background in which the common folk of the countryside and the natural world itself are so interpenetrated that we feel we might be reading a narrative poem by William Wordsworth, whose spirit hovers everywhere. Henry James, writing about *Silas Marner* and the earlier *Adam Bede,* George Eliot's first full-length novel, said that "her perception was a perception of nature much more than of art," by which he meant that both books thus displayed an artistic weakness. James was not much interested in country folk, and *Silas Marner* is very much a pastoral novel, prophesying Thomas Hardy. We learn to read *Silas Marner* as we read the Book of Ruth in the Bible, or as we mull over Wordsworth's *The Ruined Cottage* or Hardy's *The Return of the Native.* A vision of nature and its processes is as much a part of such pastoral stories as the leading characters are, and Henry James's distinction between a perception of nature and a perception of art fades away in great writings of this kind.

F. R. Leavis sensibly compared *Silas Marner* to Charles Dickens's *Hard Times,* pointing out that both were "moral fables." A moral fable presumably allows for somewhat different standards of probability than a wholly naturalistic fiction could sustain. Silas is truly a rather unlikely prospect, being a half-mad solitary, to have a deserted child deposited upon his hearth, but within the aesthetic borders of what is almost a fairy story (as Leavis observed) the substitution of little Eppie for Silas's stolen gold and dead sister is wonderfully persuasive:

> When Marner's sensibility returned, he continued the action which had been arrested, and closed his door, unaware of the chasm in his consciousness, unaware of any intermediate change, except that the light had grown dim, and that he was

chilled and faint. He thought he had been too long standing at the door and looking out. Turning towards the hearth where the two logs had fallen apart, and sent forth only a red uncertain glimmer, he seated himself on his fireside chair, and was stooping to push his logs together, when, to his blurred vision, it seemed as if there were gold on the floor in front of the hearth. Gold!—his own gold—brought back to him as mysteriously as it had been taken away! He felt his heart begin to beat violently, and for a few moments he was unable to stretch out his hand and grasp the restored treasure. The heap of gold seemed to glow and get larger beneath his agitated gaze. He leaned forward at last, and stretched forth his hand; but instead of the hard coin with the familiar resisting outline, his fingers encountered soft warm curls. In utter amazement, Silas fell on his knees and bent his head low to examine the marvel: it was a sleeping child—a round, fair thing, with soft yellow rings all over its head. Could this be his little sister come back to him in a dream—his little sister whom he carried about in his arms for a year before she died, when he was a small boy without shoes or stockings? That was the first thought that darted across Silas's blank wonderment. *Was* it a dream? He rose to his feet again, pushed his logs together, and, throwing on some dried leaves and sticks, raised a flame; but the flame did not disperse the vision—it only lit up more distinctly the little round form of the child and its shabby clothing. It was very much like his little sister.

In a fable of regeneration, like *Silas Marner,* this epiphany has extraordinary plangency and force. George Eliot's art, throughout the book, is almost flawless in its patience. The narrator's stance is one of Wordsworthian "wise passivity"; it is nature and community working slowly and silently together that regenerate Silas and that punish both Cass brothers, each in proportion to his hardness of heart. It is the same spirit, of what might be called the natural, simple heart, that is manifested by Eppie when she chooses to stay with Silas rather than return to the wealthy father who abandoned her:

> 'Thank you, ma'am—thank you, sir, for your offers—they're very great, and far above my wish. For I should have no delight in life any more if I was forced to go away from my father, and knew he was sitting at home, a-thinking of me and feeling lone. We've been used to be happy together every day, and I can't think o' no happiness without him. And he says he'd nobody i' the world till I was sent to him, and he'd have nothing when I was gone. And he's took care of me and loved me from the

first, and I'll cleave to him as long as he lives, and nobody shall ever come between him and me.'

"Cleaving" is the Biblical metaphor there and throughout *Silas Marner.* Most moral fables in literature fall away into an abstract harshness, and become rather bad books. George Eliot's genius vitalizes the fairy story or fabulistic aspect of *Silas Marner,* because of her uncanny power of humanizing all concerns of morality. In a letter to her publisher, she remarked upon "the remedial influence of pure, natural human relations," as she had sought to portray them, and then added a fine afterthought: "The Nemesis is a very mild one." ❖

Biography of George Eliot (Mary Ann Evens)

George Eliot was born Mary Ann (or Marian) Evans on November 22, 1819, in Chilvers Cotton, Warwickshire, England. Her father, Robert Evans, a former artisan, was an estate agent for wealthy local landowners. In addition to providing her with a solid education at local schools, he instilled in her strong, conservative Christian values. A serious child, Mary Ann demonstrated impressive intelligence and an ardent Evangelical piety. When her mother died, seventeen-year-old Mary Ann assumed responsibility for running the household but continued her studies in German, Italian, and music with private tutors.

Mary Ann Evans began to blossom as a true intellectual after she moved with her father to Coventry, where she encountered independent thinkers such as Harriet Martineau, Robert Owen, and Ralph Waldo Emerson. Under their influence she started to question the supernatural claims and dogma of her theological books and ultimately lost her faith in Christianity. She declared that she could no longer attend church in good conscience but relented because of her father's intense disapproval; Christian ethics would continue to guide her, but she shed the "narrow, self-delusive fanaticism" of her former evangelicalism. In 1844 she began translating D. F. Strauss's controversial German critical interpretation of the New Testament, *The Life of Jesus;* it was published anonymously in 1846.

Evans became fully independent in 1849, when her father died. After traveling through France, Italy, and Switzerland, she moved to London in 1851 to join the city's circle of avant-garde intellectuals. She worked as the assistant editor of the prestigious liberal journal *Westminster Review* and wrote many literary reviews. The position caused her some emotional stress, however, because *Westminster* publisher John Chapman's wife and mistress both expressed jealousy that Evans was boarding in Chapman's house.

Evans escaped this difficult situation but soon had to make another tough decision in her private life. She befriended and gradually fell in love with the literary critic and journalist George Henry Lewes, who because of legal complications was unable to obtain a divorce. In 1854 Evans resolved to disregard social conventions and live with Lewes as his wife. Initially considered scandalous—her brother Isaac disowned her—the deeply happy, supportive union became more accepted and lasted until Lewes's death in 1878.

It was Lewes who encouraged Evans to write fiction. After completing a translation of Spinoza's *Ethics* in 1855, she began work on the three long stories that were published as *Scenes of Clerical Life* (1858). The stories appeared in *Blackwood's Magazine* under her new pseudonym, George Eliot—"George" because it was Lewes's name and "Eliot" because it was "a good mouth-filling, easily pronounced word." (She continued using the pen name but revealed her identity when her work was wrongly attributed to a Warwickshire clergyman.) The warm, insightful stories garnered Eliot praise from critics and notable readers such as Dickens and Thackeray.

Eliot's reputation was cemented with the debut of her first novel, *Adam Bede* (1859). The popular pastoral novel established her as one of the foremost writers of the Victorian era. As she would do throughout her writing, she relied upon childhood memory and imagination to create the story and set it in a slightly earlier, more traditional England (before the Reform Act of 1832). Memories of her father inspired the character of Adam Bede, a good, hard-working peasant who falls in love with a farm girl, who is seduced by a squire. In this novel and others, Eliot stands apart from her peers with her realistic, sympathetic portrayal of the lives of ordinary people.

Eliot returned to her youth with the semi-autobiographical *The Mill on the Floss* (1860). She created one of her most compelling heroines in Maggie Tulliver, a fully drawn character who is unable to meet her potential because of the limitations placed by society. In a balanced, psychologically penetrating way, Eliot explored the relationship between individual character and the social environment.

Eliot's last rustic novel to spring from her childhood memories, *Silas Marner: The Weaver of Raveloe,* appeared in 1861. The novel depicts how a child's love saves the embittered title character. This moral fable was followed by Eliot's only historical novel, *Romola* (1863), and a political novel, *Felix Holt* (1866).

Middlemarch, Eliot's masterpiece, was serialized in 1871/72 and published in book form in 1872. In four interrelated plots, she crafted a sweeping portrait of provincial England. The characters are inextricably connected to each other and the community, and their slightest actions affect the whole. Eliot brilliantly illuminated the subtleties of character development and moral deterioration, as well as the gap between noble aspirations and realistic limitations.

Eliot published her last novel, *Daniel Deronda,* in 1876. In the contemporary story, the title character works to establish a Jewish state in Palestine. After Lewes died in 1878, Eliot devoted herself to readying his final manuscripts for publication. In May 1880 she married family friend John Walter Cross but did not live long to enjoy the union. She died in London on December 22, 1880. Her work directly influenced Thomas Hardy, D. H. Lawrence, Henry James, and many others, and she is remembered as one of England's preeminent novelists. ✦

Thematic and Structural Analysis

Despite its brevity, surface simplicity, and sentimentality, *Silas Marner,* dealing with the life of a weaver near the remote village of Raveloe, examines issues of universal human relevance as well as major social developments in nineteenth-century Britain. Hidden in a "snug well-wooded hollow, quite an hour's journey on horseback from any turnpike," Raveloe is insulated from the industrial developments transforming Victorian society. In its nostalgia for older, preindustrial rural England; focus on concrete, mundane details of rural life; and examination of the mystery and strangeness of everyday reality among country folk, *Silas Marner* picks up important threads of English romanticism. However, the novel refutes the romantic idea of the contentment and purity of the rural world: The placid beauty of the landscape does not preclude theft, intolerance, ignorance, profligacy, and inner torment. Strong feeling or the utter lack of it plays a major part in determining the events of *Silas Marner.* Eliot shows that the emotions are a source of wisdom, leading to right action and perception of truth; but the novel also concedes that the spontaneous overflow of powerful feeling can be delusive, causing inaction and tragedy.

The motif of inner growth is introduced in **chapter one**: Before he came to Raveloe, Silas's life was a "metamorphosis" of "mental activity" because of his solitary life as an artisan and his membership in "a narrow religious sect," the "little hidden world" of the church at Lantern Yard. His trusting simplicity contrasted with the self-satisfied, complacent sense of "inward triumph" of his friend William Dane, a member of the congregation who was convinced of his own salvation. Silas, who suffered cataleptic seizures, was engaged to Sarah, a young servant. Seeking to undermine Silas's relationship with Sarah, Dane alleged that Silas's trances were visitations of Satan. Sitting at the bedside of the gravely ill church deacon one night, Silas experienced a cataleptic trance, and during the trance the deacon died. The next day it was revealed that church money had been stolen from the deacon's room and

Silas's pocket knife had been found in the bureau housing the money. Dane claimed to have found the bag formerly containing the money in a chest in Silas's chamber. Silas was accused of theft, declared guilty by the congregation, and expelled. His experience showed him that "there is no just God that governs the earth righteously, but a God of lies that bears witness against the innocent."

Silas's "anguish of disappointed faith" introduces the novel's major theme, the nature of divine justice: whether human life is governed by a provident God who extends grace and shows love by directing humanity to fortuitous ends, or whether humanity is ruled by a malicious deity who leads us into misery and abandonment. *Silas Marner* also explores a corollary question, humankind's role in directing its fate: Are we entirely ruled by a higher power, be it called chance, fortune, destiny, or God? Or can we influence our destiny by making proper use of free will and free choice, individual initiative and effort, and thus achieve right action?

Chapter two focuses on Silas's "Lethean" exile. Though Raveloe's orchards are "lazy with neglected plenty" and its people live "in careless abundance," he feels cut off from the "Power in which he had vainly trusted" and believes "there [is] no Unseen Love that [cares] for him." He shrinks into a lonely, "insect-like existence," working incessantly at his loom. His eccentricities inspire fear and repulsion in the minds of the primitive country people, completing his isolation. In this void, the love of accumulating money becomes an all-consuming passion. Handling and counting his coins each night is for Silas "like the satisfaction of a thirst." As his love for his money grows, his life is narrowed to "the functions of weaving and hoarding": Without any end for his money, he is also without relationship to any living soul. His gold is a symbol of Silas himself: hard, sterile, loveless, purposeless, faithless. His love of gold advances Eliot's critique of Victorian materialism and the mercantile ethic undirected to higher ends. Silas endures this state of "withering" for fifteen years.

Chapter three introduces the second plot line of the narrative, the interactions between Squire Cass and two of his sons, Godfrey and Dunstan, who epitomize the landed gentry of the "old-fashioned country life" that is "aloof from the currents of industrial energy and Puritan earnestness." Supported by rents from tenants, Squire Cass keeps his sons "at home in idleness," allowing them and himself a life of unrelenting dissipation. Dunstan (also called Dunsey), who loves drinking and gambling, is a "spiteful, jeering fellow" who, the narrator reveals, enjoys "his drink the more when other people [go] dry."

The squire's eldest son, Godfrey, covets strong-minded Nancy Lammeter but is tormented by a secret marriage, the consequence of "low passion." Molly Farren, his wife, is addicted to opium and has borne him a child. Dunstan knows this and has been blackmailing his brother. To buy Dunstan's silence, Godfrey gave him the 100-pound rent of a tenant named Fowler, which Dunstan then squandered on drinking and gambling. Habitually short of funds, the squire now needs the rent money. To cover the embezzlement, Dunstan proposes selling Godfrey's horse, Wildfire, and reiterates his threat to expose Godfrey's marriage to gain his brother's compliance. Although Godfrey finds his plan intolerable, he fears disinheritance and losing Nancy if his marriage is revealed. Intensifying his "natural irresolution and moral cowardice," Godfrey's predicament leaves him "helpless as an uprooted tree," and he acquiesces.

In his daily pursuit of empty pleasures, Godfrey is typical of his class, whose only work is "to ride round their land, getting heavier and heavier in their saddles" and pass their remaining time in "half-listless gratification of senses dulled by monotony." Godfrey has descended beneath mere dullness, however; his dealings with his wife and brother have dragged him "into mud and slime" and deprived him of "all wholesome motive." He is most tormented by his awareness that he is the victim not of higher forces but of his own rash passions.

In **chapter four** Dunstan sells Wildfire, a sale contingent on the horse's safe delivery. After the agreement, however, he decides to ride Wildfire in the day's hunt. During the hunt Dunstan pushes his luck, takes "one fence too many," and impales Wildfire on a hedge stake. Having killed the horse, Dunstan must think of another way to replace the embezzled rent money. While walking back to Raveloe, he considers the idea of borrowing money from Silas. As night falls, the mist turns into rain and Dunstan stumbles upon Silas's cottage, which is located by a pond known as the Stone-pit. Finding the door unlocked and the cottage deserted, Dunstan decides to steal the money. He searches the cottage, finds the gold, and steps back into the dark, rainy night.

Chapter five reveals that Dunstan has been able to steal Silas's money only through luck: By chance Silas was away briefly from his dwelling that evening; by chance he left his door unlocked. Returning to his cottage, Silas wants to touch his gold. He goes to the hiding place, a hole in the cottage floor, and finds the gold missing. Overcome with terror, he feverishly searches the entire cottage before realizing that his money is gone, and he sends forth "a wild ringing scream, the cry of desolation." Looking for help, he makes his way to the Rainbow Tavern.

The patrons gathered at the Rainbow (**chapter six**)—a farrier, a tailor, a butcher, a wheelwright, an assistant parish clerk—are a cross section of Raveloe's common people. The dialogue in this chapter simulates the cadences and diction of ordinary country people, a stylistic ideal of some romantic writers. However, whereas the romantics tended to idealize rural society, Eliot does not; conversation at the Rainbow reveals dullness, crudeness, ignorance, and superstition as well as common sense and decency.

Silas, ghostlike, appears in the tavern in **chapter seven**. As he describes his plight, most of the patrons believe that the theft has been committed by a "preternatural felon" because the robber left no traces and somehow knew the precise time to strike, which would be "incalculable by mortal agents." Dowlas, the farrier, ridicules this idea, finally convincing the patrons to notify the constable and magistrate.

As the investigation proceeds (**chapter eight**), the people of Raveloe focus on a peddler who is said to have been in the area. Suspicions about the peddler are based on only one tangible clue, a tinderbox found near Silas's cottage; though there are no clear recollections of the peddler, from this one concrete detail the rustics construct a complete image of him. With irony, Eliot suggests that their deductions illustrate ignoble aspects of the rural mind—a morbid imagination, a suspicious nature, ignorant prejudices, and the need to construct simple-minded generalizations: The peddler had a "swarthy foreign-ness of complexion which boded little honesty"; the rustics wonder that he did not murder Silas, since "men of that sort, with rings in their ears, had been known for murders often."

As speculation about the theft continues, the squire's family has its own mystery to resolve: the disappearance of Dunstan. Godfrey learns that Dunstan has destroyed Wildfire. Although he hopes that his brother will not return, Godfrey is certain that Dunstan has escaped the accident unharmed because "he'll never be hurt—he's made to hurt other people." Godfrey debates whether to confess his secret marriage and the embez-zlement of the rent money, but he fears the squire's violent temper and unrelenting "fierce severity" and decides not to confess but to wait and "rely on chances which might be favorable."

Eliot's portrait of the gentry becomes satire in **chapter nine**. Squire Cass, habitually slovenly in dress, exhibits the authorita-tiveness of a man who "thought of superiors as remote exis-tences." The squire has been "used to homage . . . all his life" and assumes that "everything that [is] his [is] the oldest and best," an opinion that goes unchallenged because he never associates "with any gentry higher than himself."

Godfrey, who has modified his decision to conceal his mis-deeds, lingers after breakfast to broach the subject. After Squire Cass feeds the deerhound Fleet enough beef "to make a poor man's holiday dinner," Godfrey confesses that he collected the 100 pounds from Fowler but gave the money to Dunstan, who squandered it. Wildfire was to be sold to cover the funds but has been destroyed, and Dunstan is missing. Enraged, the squire declares that his son is "a shilly-shally fellow" incapable of making both his legs "walk one way" and needs marriage to Nancy Lammeter to correct his life. If Godfrey does not pro-pose marriage, the squire will do it for him. Confused and dreading the possibility of betrothal to one woman while mar-ried to another, Godfrey flees to his usual refuge, hoping that an "unforeseen turn of fortune, some favorable chance" will save him.

Investigation of the theft of Silas's gold stumbles along in **chapter ten**. The mysterious peddler is discounted, and no one connects Dunstan with the robbery that occurred on the day of his disappearance. Silas, meanwhile, is "feeling the withering desolation of [his] bereavement" over the lost gold. The prospect of handling his gold gone, the evening brings "no phantasm of delight to still the poor soul's craving," and the idea of new earnings is "only a fresh reminder of his loss." He spends his life in his cottage, moaning "like one in pain."

Silas receives kind treatment from the people of Raveloe, some of whom even call at his cottage to cheer him—though their visits at first produce little comfort. Eliot introduces a new theme, that tragedy engenders growth of insight, specifically the awareness of one's need of other people. Silas realizes that, if he is to be helped, "it must come from without"; seeing people inspires a "consciousness of dependence on their goodwill." His principal benefactor is Dolly Winthrop, the wheelwright's wife. With simple piety and a sincere desire to comfort, Dolly exhorts him to attend church at Christmas. But love of humanity and faith in God are still dead in him. Winter is a symbol of his pain, deadness of spirit, and sense of persecution by the universe: The "black frost" presses "cruelly on every blade of grass"; the snow imprisons him within misery and solitude.

While Silas is controlled by the demon of depression, Godfrey Cass is plagued by another demon, anxiety about exposure of his secret marriage, by either Dunstan or the intrusion of his wife.

In **chapter eleven** the torments of Godfrey and Silas contrast with the mirth of Squire Cass's New Year's Eve celebration at his estate, the Red House. Beneath the merriment and opulence, petty snobbery, crudeness, and obsessive preoccupation with trivial concerns abound.

When she arrives at the Red House, Nancy Lammeter—fastidious, high-minded, and inflexible—is pained by thoughts of Godfrey's inconsistent attentions and moral waywardness; she is also troubled by his continued pursuit of her even though she has made clear her determination not to marry him. Having the necessary attributes of a lady—veracity, honor, deference, refinement, constancy—she will not be led by "dazzling rank" into marriage with someone irresponsible. During the party, however, Godfrey is overcome with "blind feeling" and begs Nancy's forgiveness, pledging to end his bad habits. Exerting the "very pressure of emotion" upon her, he begins to break down her resistance.

Meanwhile, Godfrey's wife trudges through snow-covered lanes toward Raveloe with her child in her arms (**chapter twelve**). In a "premeditated act of vengeance," Molly seeks to expose his marriage and paternity to the squire and his guests celebrating at the Red House. She is bitter at Godfrey's neglect, even though she knows that her misery is caused by her own enslavement to "the demon Opium." Similarly, she, not chance or a higher power, determines her present fate: In her indolence, Molly has journeyed at a slow pace until, oppressed by the cold and darkness, she needs comfort; knowing "but one comforter," she takes a long draft of laudanum (an opium preparation), choosing oblivion from aching weariness over the dictates of a mother's love. As she flings away the empty vial, emblematic of her life, a freezing wind arises and she yields to "a supreme immediate longing that curtained off all futurity— the longing to lie down and sleep."

Molly's child awakens and, attracted by a bright light emanating from a nearby dwelling, toddles through the open door of Silas's cottage and seats herself by the blazing fire. Silas has developed the habit of opening the door to look out in the hope that his money might be "somehow coming back to him." By chance, this evening the door is open for a long period after he is overcome by "the invisible wand of catalepsy." Awakening from the trance, he believes that he sees his gold restored on the floor in front of the fire. The glowing heap of gold, upon inspection, is the soft yellow hair of the sleeping child. Sight of the child inspires tender feelings and his "presentiment of some Power presiding over his life."

In **chapter thirteen,** Silas intrudes upon Squire Cass's party, carrying the child. His entrance is the pivotal episode in the development of a primary theme, the interconnectedness of humanity: The good fortune or dire circumstances of one individual inevitably bring about the happiness or distress of others. Godfrey's embezzlement leads to Dunstan's impaling Wildfire, which leads to the theft of Silas's gold; Molly's death brings the child to Silas; both events will have an incalculable effect on Godfrey. When the search for the child's mother begins, Godfrey, terrified that Molly may be alive, again contemplates admitting his secret marriage and paternity; however, he does not have the courage. Soon a young woman, "some vagrant—quite in rags," is found dead in the snow. Godfrey's future is secured, but so is Silas's.

Molly's death has "the force of destiny" on "certain human lives . . . shaping their joys and sorrows even to the end." Silas raises her child, causing the people of Raveloe to feel greater sympathy for him (**chapter fourteen**). He believes that the child, whom he names Eppie, is a gift from Providence. On the advice of Dolly Winthrop, Silas has Eppie baptized, which increases his connectedness with humanity: Whereas gold intensified his alienation, the child, in her need to embrace the world, creates "fresh links" between his life and the people of Raveloe. The child influences the growth of the adult: By calling him away from his weaving, Eppie forces his thoughts "onward" to new objects. She reawakens his senses and inspires hope, purpose, and joy in him. She links "him once more with the whole world." Their relationship implies that what is truly priceless is love and the bonds between people. Godfrey is also regenerated: Free from a vengeful wife and a diabolical brother, he can shape a new life for himself. Accordingly, he chooses to become "a reformed man" (**chapter fifteen**).

In **chapter sixteen**, the narrative resumes sixteen years later. Godfrey, now forty and the squire, is married to Nancy. He discreetly provides for the needs of Silas (now fifty-five) and Eppie (now eighteen). In seeking what was necessary for Eppie, Silas has accepted the customs and beliefs of Raveloe. Connecting his new joy with his previous religious faith, he has gained a "sense of presiding goodness."

Having protected Eppie from "the lowering influences of village talk and habits," Silas has preserved in her the "freshness which is sometimes falsely supposed to be an invariable attribute of rusticity." Because "perfect love . . . can exalt the relations of the least-instructed human beings," she has developed "a touch of refinement and fervor which came from no other teaching than that of tenderly-nurtured unvitiated feeling."

The yellow flowers of the furze bush upon which Molly died, transplanted in the new garden near Silas's cottage, sustain the bright yellow imagery that connects stages of *Silas Marner*. After the negative association with Silas's hoard of gold, imagery of yellow brightness has positive associations: The gleaming fire that attracted the child to Silas's cottage, Eppie's golden locks, and the yellow furze bush imply growth, meaningful existence, and perceptual illumination. While snow is a symbol of death and inward desolation, the background for Silas's alienation and a cause of Eppie's mother's death, water now is a prominent ambiguous symbol. The Stone-pit, the pond near Silas's cottage, is being drained in Godfrey's land-reclamation project. Although the pond is a place of death, its draining implies movement to new life and change, whose power Silas recognizes when he says, "[T]hings *will* change, whether we like it or not."

On a quiet Sunday afternoon, Nancy sits alone in the Red House and contemplates her years with Godfrey (**chapter seventeen**). Her thoughts focus on the "one main thread of painful experience in her married life," their childlessness. Six years earlier, and then again four years earlier, Godfrey had proposed adopting Eppie. Now Nancy wonders whether she had been right to deny her husband's wish. After replaying the discussions in her mind, she concludes that, however painful the decision might have been for Godfrey and for her, she was correct. Her tenacious beliefs have evolved into a rigid code with which she strictly regulates her life. She believes in accepting Providence and in the wrongness of trying to change one's lot. Having tried to have children and failed, she concludes that for her, parenthood is "not meant to be." Her views are simplistic, superstitious metaphysics: While acknowledging the ultimate supremacy of divine will, *Silas Marner* suggests that human life is determined by the interplay between Providence and humankind's choices and actions.

Godfrey's arguments for adopting Eppie, which Nancy recalls, reflect the insensitivity, arrogance, and lack of empathy of his class: The weaver would surely want the best for the child and would be glad of her good fortune; it is "an appropriate thing for people in a higher station to take a charge off the hands of a man in a lower." It never occurs to him that a poor man like Silas would rather die than part with his child, that "deep affections" can exist with "callous palms and scant means." Still averse to facing difficult situations, Godfrey is yet unable to reveal that Eppie is his daughter by his secret marriage. Moreover, his guilty conscience makes him see his childlessness as retribution for not acknowledging Eppie.

With the Stone-pit completely drained in **chapter eighteen**, the skeletal remains of Dunstan (identifiable by his watch and seals and by Godfrey's hunting whip) are discovered, along with the gold Dunstan had stolen from Silas. Godfrey, realizing that everything "comes to light . . . sooner or later," confesses to Nancy that Eppie is his child by Molly, and they resolve to adopt her.

In **chapter nineteen**, with his recovered gold stacked on a table in the cottage, Silas tells Eppie how her arrival gradually transformed his desolate life. Before, his money had been his only joy. After he lost it and she appeared, he believed at times that Eppie might be turned back into the lost gold, and, he says, "I thought I should be glad if I could feel it, and find it was come back." But as his love for her grew, he "should have thought it was a curse come again, if it had drove you from me. . . . You didn't know then, Eppie . . . what your old father felt for you." "But I know now, father," Eppie responds. "If it hadn't been for you . . . there'd have been nobody to love me." Silas observes that their lives are wonderful and that money has no power over him now, but that if he lost Eppie he would feel forsaken again and might "lose the feeling that God was good."

A knock on the door interrupts their conversation, and Godfrey and Nancy enter. After exchanging pleasantries, Godfrey proposes to adopt Eppie, arguing that he and his wife would better provide for her and would "make a lady of her," for which she is "more fit . . . than for a rough life"; her elevation, Godfrey declares, would "comfort" Silas. Despite painful emotions, Silas states that he will not stand in the way of

Eppie's happiness. But Eppie declares that she cannot leave her father. Undeterred, Godfrey reveals that he is Eppie's biological father. This "natural claim," he maintains, supersedes every other. But Silas responds that God gave Eppie to him when Godfrey abandoned her, and Silas is the only father she has ever known. Godfrey asks him to consider "the thing more reasonably," implies Silas's selfishness in opposing Eppie's welfare, and insists on his "duty" to care for Eppie to prevent her marrying "some low working-man." Fearing that he may have selfish motives, Silas wants Eppie to decide her fate. Eppie doubts she could feel any happiness without Silas and declares, "I'll cleave to him as long as he lives, and nobody shall ever come between him and me." Further, she says, she prefers "the working-folks, and their houses, and their ways" and intends to marry a workingman. Godfrey and Nancy leave.

Recognizing that "there's debts we can't pay like money debts," Godfrey abandons the plan to adopt Eppie but nonetheless pledges to assist her in the life she has chosen (**chapter twenty**). Because he believes nothing good could come of it, he promises Nancy that he will not publicly reveal he is Eppie's father.

In **chapter twenty-one** Silas returns to Lantern Yard with Eppie to learn whether his innocence in the deacon's robbery has been determined. Lantern Yard has become "a great manufacturing town." Eppie finds it "a dark, ugly place" that "hides the sky"; troubled by "begrimed faces" gazing out from a gloomy doorway, she feels "stifled" and wonders how people can live packed "so close together." Silas is distressed by the disappearance of the religious community, in whose place stands a large factory. Now he will never know whether the truth about the robbery has been discovered and whether his name has been cleared. His experience in the new Lantern Yard symbolizes the dislocations—of certitude, inner peace, and bonds with the past—perpetrated by the Industrial Revolution.

On the morning of the wedding of Eppie and Dolly Winthrop's son Aaron (the **conclusion**), sunshine falls on "old-fashioned gardens" that display their "golden and purple wealth." Attired in pure white that makes her hair seem like a "dash of gold on a lily," Eppie joins hands with her husband and Silas while Dolly walks closely behind with her husband. Though Godfrey is away, the rest of Raveloe anticipates the wedding feast that he has provided at the Rainbow Inn. The assembled company discuss how Silas "brought a blessing on himself" when he took in Eppie. This idea meets "no contradiction" because when a man "deserved his good luck, it was the part of his neighbors to wish him joy." At the cottage, Eppie's garden flourishes, and its flowers shine "with answering gladness" as the wedding party approaches.

Though Eliot has shown that rural life may hold pernicious realities, *Silas Marner* concludes with an Edenic vision of the rural world as a garden containing benevolent nature, a comfortable life, gradual change within a framework of permanence and order, and, most importantly, loving community. Presented as an example of the life of peace and harmony that the Almighty bestows on those who conduct their lives with kind, loving hearts, the closing portrait is also a social ideal amid the disruption and bleakness brought by the Industrial Revolution. ❖

—*Edward Dramin*
Iona College

List of Characters

Silas Marner is an eccentric linen-weaver who, after being wrongly accused of theft and expelled from the religious community at Lantern Yard, leads a solitary life in the English countryside near the village of Raveloe. Alienated, prone to cataleptic trances, and having knowledge of herbal medicine, Silas is believed by the country people to possess powers of magic and is thus feared and scorned. By working incessantly and living frugally, he amasses a considerable pile of gold—the one love of his life and the center of his universe after his expulsion. His miserliness warps his mind, destroys his imagination, restricts his perception of the world, and diminishes his spirit. Soon, however, a baby girl wanders into his cottage on a snowy night. Silas raises the child, whom he names Eppie, in love and complete devotion, thus eventually dissipating his misery over his lost gold. In the process he becomes connected with his neighbors and reconciled with the world.

Eppie is the child who wanders from her dying mother toward the warm yellow glow emanating from Silas's hearth. Adorned with golden locks, she replaces Silas's gold as a source of true value. Under his loving care she develops into a beautiful, virtuous woman. Eppie's devotion to Silas is boundless: When her real father appears after many years to claim her, she chooses to stay with Silas rather than enjoy a life of upper-class affluence.

Godfrey Cass, the eldest son of the local squire, epitomizes the idle, lazy rural gentry and is dedicated to cards, drinking, and hunting. His main traits are vacillation and irresolution. Coveting well-born, high-minded Nancy Lammeter, Godfrey is Eppie's father through his secret marriage to the lowly Molly Farren. When Molly is found dead in the snow, Godfrey undergoes a moral transformation, discards his profligate ways, and marries Nancy. After providing for some of the material needs of Eppie and Silas for sixteen years, he resolves to claim Eppie as his daughter but is thwarted by the deep bonds she and Silas have formed.

Dunstan Cass, Godfrey's brother, is a dissolute rogue. He blackmails his brother into giving him the rent money Godfrey collected from a tenant; after squandering the money, he coerces Godfrey into letting him sell Godfrey's prize horse to replace the embezzled funds. But before the horse can be delivered to its buyer, Dunstan accidentally impales it on a hedge stake. Later that night he stumbles upon Silas Marner's cottage and decides to steal Silas's gold. After the theft, his vision obscured by mist and rain, Dunstan falls into the nearby pond, the Stone-pit, and drowns.

Squire Cass exemplifies the sloth, self-centeredness, and indulgence in material pleasures of the rural squirearchy of the mid-Victorian period. Obtuse, neglectful, and slovenly, he presides over run-down lands, a sloppy house, and decadent sons. Possessing his class's obsession to perpetuate shallow appearances and the family line, the squire unrelentingly prods Godfrey to propose to Nancy Lammeter.

Nancy Lammeter, the beautiful woman whom Godfrey Cass courts and marries, has a stalwart moral sense and is uncompromising in her principles. She thus rejects Godfrey's early proposal and even his attentions because of his moral waywardness. When he later reforms, she marries him. The match is appropriate because she possesses qualities her husband lacks—truthfulness, common sense, and refinement. Unmaterialistic and introspective, she rigidly believes in accepting divine will, and because she believes it is God's will that their marriage be childless, she initially denies Godfrey's wish to adopt a child.

Molly Farren is the opium-addicted, lowborn woman to whom Godfrey is secretly married and the mother of Eppie. Virtually abandoned by Godfrey, she sets out for Squire Cass's New Year's celebration with Eppie, intending to expose Godfrey there. But after taking a long draft of opium, she falls asleep in the snow and dies.

Dolly Winthrop, the wife of the town wheelwright, befriends Silas after the loss of his gold and offers him advice on how to raise Eppie. Exemplifying simple rural piety, she reaffirms the ultimate benevolence and justice of God's ways and encourages Silas and Eppie to participate in the rituals and ceremonies of the church in Raveloe.

William Dane is Silas's devious, hypocritical friend in the religious community at Lantern Yard. Convinced of his own special election to salvation, Dane covets Silas's fiancée, Sarah, and asserts that Silas's cataleptic trances are signs of demonic possession. He plants evidence incriminating Silas in the theft of church funds and is a leading accuser.

Sarah is the young servant engaged to marry Silas during his earlier life at Lantern Yard. She rejects him when he is accused of theft and soon marries William Dane. ❖

Critical Views

[George Eliot discussed the writing of *Silas Marner* with her publisher in a letter written in 1861. Here she states that the story, while somber, is not meant to be sad and that the inspiration for it came to her when as a child she saw a linen-weaver with a bag on his back.]

I don't wonder at your finding my story, as far as you have read it, rather sombre: indeed, I should not have believed that any one would have been interested in it but myself (since William Wordsworth is dead) if Mr. Lewes had not been strongly arrested by it. But I hope you will not find it at all a sad story, as a whole, since it sets—or is intended to set—in a strong light the remedial influences of pure, natural human relations. The Nemesis is a very mild one. I have felt all through as if the story would have lent itself best to metrical rather than prose fiction, especially in all that relates to the psychology of Silas; except that, under that treatment, there could not be an equal play of humour. It came to me first of all, quite suddenly, as a sort of legendary tale, suggested by my recollection of having once, in early childhood, seen a linen-weaver with a bag on his back; but, as my mind dwelt on the subject, I became inclined to a more realistic treatment.

My chief reason for wishing to publish the story now, is, that I like my writings to appear in the order in which they are written, because they belong to successive mental phases, and when they are a year behind me, I can no longer feel that thorough identification with them which gives zest to the sense of authorship. I generally like them better at that distance, but then, I feel as if they might just as well have been written by somebody else.

—George Eliot, Letter to John Blackwood (24 February 1861), *The George Eliot Letters,* ed. Gordon S. Haight (New Haven: Yale University Press, 1954), Vol. 3, pp. 382–83

[*Silas Marner* received uniformly praiseworthy reviews upon its appearance in the spring of 1861. In this review from the *Saturday Review* (London), the anonymous critic praises Eliot for the compactness of the novel and its sensitive depiction of humble life.]

The highest tribute that can be paid to this book may be paid it very readily. It is as good as *Adam Bede*, except that it is shorter. And that an author should be able to produce a series of works so good in so very peculiar a style, is as remarkable as anything that has occurred in the history of English literature in this century. The plot of *Silas Marner* is good, and the delineation of character is excellent. But other writers who have the power of story-telling compose plots as interesting, and perhaps sketch characters as well. It is in the portraiture of the poor, and of what it is now fashionable to call "the lower middle class," that this writer is without a rival, and no phase of life could be harder to draw. A person with observation and humour might give a sketch of one or two sets of poor people, and of village farmers and carpenters, but the sketches he could give would be limited by his personal observation. George Eliot alone moves among this unknown, and to most people unknowable, section of society as if quite at home there, and can let imagination run loose and disport itself in a field that, we think, has been only very partially opened even to the best writers. Sir Walter Scott drew a few pictures of humble Scotch life, and none of his creations won him more deserved reputation than the characters of Andrew Fairservice and Caleb Balderstone, and the scenes among the poor fishing population in *The Antiquary*. But, good as these sketches were, they were very limited. We soon got to an end of them; but in *Silas Marner*, the whole book, or nearly the whole book, is made up of such scenes. The writer can picture what uneducated villagers think and say, and can reproduce on paper the picture which imagination has suggested. The gift is so special, the difficulty is so great, the success is so complete, that the works of George Eliot come on us as a new revelation of what society in quiet English parishes really is and has been. How hard it is to draw the poor may easily be seen if we turn to the ordinary tales of country life that are written in such abundance by ladies. There the poor are always looked at from the point of view of the rich. They are so many subjects for experimenting on, for reclaiming, improving, being anxious about, and relieving. They have no existence apart from the presence of a curate and a district visitor. They live in order to take tracts and broth. This is a very natural, and in some degree a very proper view for the well-intentioned rich to take of the poor. It is right that those who have spiritual and temporal blessings should care for the souls and bodies of those around them. But the poor remain, during the process and in its description, as a distinct race. What they think of and do when they are not being improved and helped, remains a blank. Those, too, who are above the reach of occasional destitution are entirely omitted from these portraitures of village life. Everyone is agreed that it would be impertinent to improve a man who gets anything like a pound a week. When, therefore, George Eliot describes the whole of a village, from the simple squire down to the wheelwright and his wife, the ground thus occupied is virgin soil.

—Unsigned, [Review of *Silas Marner*], *Saturday Review* (London), 13 April 1861, pp. 369–70

E. S. DALLAS ON CHANCE IN *SILAS MARNER*

[E. S. Dallas (1828–1879) was a British literary critic best known for the critical work *The Gay Science* (1866). In this review of *Silas Marner,* Dallas finds that, in contrast to Eliot's previous work, this novel relies perhaps too heavily on chance to move the plot forward.]

In Mr. Wilkie Collins's last novel ⟨*The Woman in White*⟩ the chief interest centres around two half-witted women in succession. Events occur which by no possibility could have happened had these women been in full possession of their senses. But in a novel which claims our attention chiefly for the intricacy of its plot, and slightly for the evolution of its characters, we almost forget the blank unsatisfactory nature of the leading personages in thinking of the startling incidents that crowd upon our notice. The interest of George Eliot's tales resting upon a different foundation, does not admit of such handling. In her stories, the characters are all in all; the incidents are of secondary importance, and grow out of the characters; a hero whose mind is nearly a blank, and whose life is represented as the sport of chance, is at variance with the spirit of her books. This will be evident if we state what are the two critical incidents in the life of Silas Marner. He was a young man of exemplary life and ardent faith, and belonged to a little flock of Methodists, assembling in a small back street, who regarded him with peculiar interest 'ever since he had fallen at a prayer meeting into a mysterious rigidity and suspension of consciousness, which, lasting for an hour or more, had been mistaken for death.' One night, while he was watching by the side of a dying deacon, he fell into one of these fits, and during his unconsciousness the deacon not only died, but also was robbed. Here is the first introduction of chance into the story. The weaver is accused of the robbery, and his Methodist friends determine to find out the guilty man, not by investigation, but by the drawing of lots. Chance upon chance—the lot fell upon Silas Marner, who goes forth and settles in the parish of Raveloe, a blighted being. At Raveloe he lives a lonely life for 15 years, at the end of which he falls into one of his trances, and on recovering his consciousness finds a little gold-haired child sleeping on his hearth. This is the second great chance of his life. As in one fit of unconsciousness he lost his all, so in another fit of unconsciousness he obtained a recompense. In either case he was helpless, had nothing to do with his own fate, and was a mere feather in the wind of chance. From this point forward in the tale, however, there is no more chance— all is work and reward, cause and effect, the intelligent mind shaping its own destiny. The honest man bestows kindness upon the child, and reaps the benefit of it in his own increasing happiness, quickened intelligence, and social position. Only this is but a very small portion of the tale, so small that, seeing the importance of it, remembering the prominence which is given to it by means of the motto on the title-page, and knowing that the spirit of it more accords with George Eliot's artistic genius than that portion of the volume which occupies the greater number of pages, we have been forced to the conjecture that the story is not what the author originally intended it to be, but is huddled up at the end.

—E. S. Dallas, [Review of Silas Marner], The Times (London), 29 April 1861, p. 12

HENRY JAMES ON THE CHARACTERS IN SILAS MARNER

[Henry James (1843–1916), perhaps the most significant American novelist of his time, was also an occasional critic. He was the author of many book reviews and critical essays, which were assembled in such volumes as French Poets and Novelists (1878), Views and Reviews (1908), Notes on Novelists (1914), and others. In this extract, James notes the formal perfection of Silas Marner as well as its convincingly realistic characters.]

To a certain extent, I think "Silas Marner" holds a higher place than any of the author's works. It is more nearly a masterpiece; it has more of that simple, rounded, consummate aspect, that absence of loose ends and gaping issues, which marks a classical work. What was attempted in it, indeed, was within more immediate reach than the heart-trials of Adam Bede and Maggie Tulliver. A poor, dull-witted, disappointed Methodist cloth-weaver; a little golden-haired foundling child; a well-meaning, irresolute country squire, and his patient, childless wife;—these, with a chorus of simple, beer-loving villagers, make up the dramatis personæ. More than any of its brother-works, "Silas Marner," I think, leaves upon the mind a deep impression of the grossly material life of agricultural England in the last days of the old régime,—the days of full-orbed Toryism, of Trafalgar and of Waterloo, when the invasive spirit of French domination threw England back upon a sense of her own insular solidity, and made her for the time doubly, brutally, morbidly English. Perhaps the best pages in the work are the first thirty, telling the story of poor Marner's disappointments in friendship and in love, his unmerited disgrace, and his long, lonely twilight-life at Raveloe, with the sole companionship of his loom, in which his muscles moved "with such even repetition, that their pause seemed almost as much a constraint as the holding of his breath." Here, as in all George Eliot's books, there is a middle life and a low life; and here, as usual, I prefer the low life. In "Silas Marner," in my opinion, she has come nearest the mildly rich tints of brown and gray, the mellow lights and the undreadful corner-shadows of the Dutch masters whom she emulates. ⟨. . .⟩

Mrs. Winthrop, the wheelwright's wife who, out of the fulness of her charity, comes to comfort Silas in the season of his distress, is in her way one of the most truthfully sketched of the author's figures. "She was in all respects a woman of scrupulous conscience, so eager for duties that life seemed to offer them too scantily unless she rose at half past four, though this threw a scarcity of work over the more advanced hours of the morning, which it was a constant problem for her to remove. . . . She was a very mild, patient woman, whose nature it was to seek out all the sadder and more serious elements of life and pasture her mind upon them." She stamps I. H. S. on her cakes and loaves without knowing what the letters mean, or indeed without knowing that they are letters, being very much surprised that Marner can "read 'em off,"—chiefly because they are on the pulpit cloth at church. She touches upon religious themes in a manner to make the superficial reader apprehend that she cultivates some polytheistic form of faith,—extremes meet. She urges Marner to go to church, and describes the satisfaction which she herself derives from the performance of her religious duties.

"If you've niver had no church, there's no telling what good it'll do you. For I feel as set up and comfortable as niver was, when I've been and heard the prayers and the singing to the praise and glory o' God, as Mr. Macey gives out,—and Mr. Crackenthorp saying good words and more partic'lar on Sacramen' day; and if a bit o' trouble comes, I feel as I can put up wi' it, for I've looked for help i' the right quarter, and giv myself up to Them as we must all give ourselves up to at the last: and if we've done our part, it is n't to be believed as Them as are above us 'ud be worse nor we are, and come short o' Theirn."

"The plural pronoun," says the author, "was no heresy of Dolly's, but only her way of avoiding a presumptuous familiarity." I imagine that there is in no other English novel a figure so simple in its elements as this of Dolly Winthrop, which is so real without being contemptible, and so quaint without being ridiculous.

—Henry James, "The Novels of George Eliot," *Atlantic Monthly* 18, No. 1 (October 1866): 482, 484–85

LESLIE STEPHEN ON WIT IN *SILAS MARNER*

[Leslie Stephen (1832–1904), the father of Virginia Woolf, was one of the leading critics of his time. Among his works are *Hours in a Library* (1874–79), *History of English Thought in the Eighteenth Century* (1876), and *Alexander Pope* (1900). In this extract from his monograph on George Eliot, Stephen notes the surprising amount of wit, humor, and satire in *Silas Marner.*]

Silas Marner, as it turned out, was to be the last work in which George Eliot was to draw an idealised portrait of her earliest circle. It is full of admirable sketches from the squire to the poor weaver; and the famous scene at the "Rainbow" is perhaps the best specimen of her humour. The condescending parish clerk and the judicious landlord and the contradictious farrier, with their discussions of village traditions, their attempts at humour, and the curious mental processes which take the place of reasoning, are delicious and inimitable. One secret is that we can sympathise with their humble attempts at intellectual intercourse. The brutality which too often underlies a good deal of more refined satire comes out in the "unflinching frankness," which at the "Rainbow" is taken for the "most piquant form of joke." The presumption of the assistant clerk, who hopes that he may have his own opinion of his vocal performances, is tempered by the remark that "there'd be two opinions about a cracked bell if the bell could hear itself," and finally crushed by the critic who tells him that his voice is "well enough when he keeps it up in his nose." It's your inside "as is n't right made for music; it's no better nor a hollow stalk."

Much of the wit that passes current in more elegant circles differs from this, less in substance, than in the skill with which the sarcasm is ostensibly veiled. When Charles Lamb proposed to examine the bumps on the skull of an illiterate person, he was just as rude, though his rudeness is allowed to pass for harmless fun. The crude attempts of the natural man are redeemed from brutality by the absence of real ill-nature. So the argument as to reality of ghostly phenomena is a tacit parody upon a good deal of the controversy roused by "Psychical research." Some people, as the landlord urges, could n't see ghosts, "not if they stood as plain as a pikestaff before 'em." My wife, as he points out, "can't smell, not if she'd the strongest of cheese under her nose. I never see a ghost myself; but then I says to myself, very like I have n't got the smell for 'em. I mean, putting a ghost for a smell, or else contrairiways. And so, I'm for holding with both sides." The farrier retorts by asking, "What's the smell got to do with it? Did ever a ghost give a man a black eye? That's what I should like to know. If ghos'es want me to believe in 'em, let 'em leave off skulking in the dark, and i' lone places—let 'em come in company and candles." "As if ghos'es 'ud want to be believed in by anybody so ignirant!" replies the parish clerk. We have read something very like this, only expressed in the "big words" which Mrs. Winthrop left to the parson. One touch of blundering makes the whole world kin; and in these good people, with their primitive views of logic and repartee and their quaint theology, we may, if we please, see a satire upon their betters. Rather, if we accept George Eliot's view, we have a kindly sympathy for the old order upon which she looked back so fondly. A modern "realist" would, I suppose, complain that she had omitted, or touched too slightly for his taste, a great many repulsive and brutal elements in the rustic world. The portraits, indeed, are so vivid as to convince us of their fidelity; but she has selected the less ugly, and taken the point of view from which we see mainly what was wholesome and kindly in the little village community. *Silas Marner* is a masterpiece in this way, and scarcely equalled in English literature, unless by Mr. Hardy's rustics in *Far from the Madding Crowd* and other early works.

—Leslie Stephen, *George Eliot* (London: Macmillan, 1902), pp. 108–10

F. R. LEAVIS ON THE ENCHANTMENT OF *SILAS MARNER*

[F. R. Leavis (1895–1978), a fellow of Downing College, Cambridge, was one of the leading literary critics of his age. He founded and edited the journal *Scrutiny* and wrote *New Bearings in English Poetry* (1932), *Revaluation* (1936), and *The Common Pursuit* (1952). In this extract from his celebrated study, *The Great Tradition* (1948), Leavis comments on the atmo-sphere of enchantment in *Silas Marner*.]

The success of *Silas Marner,* that charming minor masterpiece, is conditioned by the absence of personal immediacy; it is a success of reminiscent and enchanted re-creation: *Silas Marner* has in it, in its solid way, something of the fairy-tale. That 'solid' presents itself because of the way in which the moral fable is realized in terms of a substantial real world. But this, though re-seen through adult experience, is the world of child-hood and youth—the world as directly known then, and what is hardly distinguishable from that, the world as known through family reminiscence, conveyed in anecdote and fireside history. The mood of enchanted adult reminiscence blends with the re-captured traditional aura to give the world of *Silas Marner* its atmosphere. And it is this atmosphere that conditions the success of the moral intention. We take this intention quite seri-ously, or, rather, we are duly affected by a realized moral signif-icance; the whole history has been conceived in a profoundly and essentially moral imagination. But the atmosphere pre-cludes too direct a reference to our working standards of prob-ability—that is, to our everyday sense of how things happen; so that there is an answer to Leslie Stephen when he com-ments on *Silas Marner* in its quality of moral fable:

> The supposed event—the moral recovery of a nature reduced by injustice and isolation to the borders of sanity—strikes one perhaps as more pretty than probable. At least, if one had to dispose of a deserted child, the experiment of dropping it by the cottage of a solitary in the hope that he would bring it up to its advantage and to his own regeneration would hardly be tried by a judicious philanthropist.

Leslie Stephen, of course, is really concerned to make a limit-ing judgment, that which is made in effect when he says:

> But in truth the whole story is conceived in a way which
> makes a pleasant conclusion natural and harmonious.

There is nothing that strikes us as false about the story; its charm depends upon our being convinced of its moral truth. But in our description of the satisfaction got from it, 'charm' remains the significant word.

The force of the limiting implication may be brought out by a comparative reference to another masterpiece of fiction that it is natural to bring under the head of 'moral fable': Dickens's *Hard Times*. The heightened reality of that great book has in it nothing of the fairy-tale, and is such as to preclude pleasantness altogether; the satisfaction given depends on a moral significance that can have no relations with charm. But the comparison is, of course, unfair: *Hard Times* has a large and complex theme, involving its author's profoundest response to contemporary civilization, while *Silas Marner* is modestly conscious of its minor quality.

The unfairness may be compensated by taking up Leslie Stephen's suggestion that '*Silas Marner* . . . scarcely equalled in English literature, unless by Mr. Hardy's rustics in *Far from the Madding Crowd* and other early works'. Actually, the comparison is to George Eliot's advantage (enormously so), and to Hardy's detriment, in ways already suggested. The praises that have been give to George Eliot for the talk at the Rainbow are deserved. It is indeed remarkable that a woman should have been able to present so convincingly an exclusively masculine *milieu*. It is the more remarkable when we recall the deplorable Bob Jakin of *The Mill on the Floss*, who is so obviously and embarrassingly a feminine product.

Silas Marner closes the first phase of George Eliot's creative life. She finds that, if she is to go on being a novelist, it must be one of a very different kind. And *Romola*, her first attempt to achieve the necessary inventiveness, might well have justified the conviction that her creative life was over.

—F. R. Leavis, *The Great Tradition: George Eliot, Henry James, Joseph Conrad* (London: Chatto & Windus, 1948), pp. 46–47

❖

ROBERT B. HEILMAN ON THE THEME AND STRUCTURE OF
SILAS MARNER

[Robert B. Heilman (b. 1906), formerly a professor of
English at the University of Washington, is the author of
Tragedy and Melodrama (1968) and *Magic in the Web:
Action and Language in Othello* (1977). In this extract,
Heilman examines the structure and some implicit
themes in *Silas Marner*.]

Beneath the Explicit surface various undercurrents amplify
theme and complicate structure. There is a regular though
quiet movement of contrasts and resemblances. Silas and
Godfrey are formally contrasted: the miser and the prodigal;
the frantic worker and the loose idler; both outside the normal
community, one in a too "closed" life, one in a too "open" life;
yet both needing love, one to open his life, the other to give it
some order. The coldly malicious William Dane and the "spiteful, jeering" Dunstann are similar embodiments of evil, both
with resemblances to Iago; yet one flourishes in conventional
dissoluteness, the other in stringent piousness; the ill disposed
man works through whatever forms of life his immediate society offers. Besides the poles of chapel and tavern there are the
poles of rationality and superstition, which appear in standard
opposition in the conflicting theories about the robbery of Silas,
but which, ironically, can move in the same way: the rational
Dane accuses Silas of commerce with the devil, and the superstitious in Raveloe suspect him of the same unholy dealings. In
Dane, of course, we see the man of calculation archetypally
exploiting the superstition of others. He can do it because of a
habit of mind that Eliot suggests is almost universal. The parish-
ioners in Lantern Yard cast lots to determine truth; Nancy
Lammeter, of far less restricted background, is equally sure that
she knows the "will of Providence" and governs her marriage
accordingly.

In the plain story of village life Eliot characteristically finds the
universal. In Silas's hoarding she finds a relationship that is in
the language itself—the relationship between *misery* and
miserliness. Wretchedness makes the miser; he suffers less
from a vice than from a disease, and the disease is the result of
an injury ("a trauma," as we now say). Furthermore, we are

forced to see the disease as representative rather than unique. Silas is compared with prisoners who fall into a kind of compulsive doodling, with researchers and theorists whose work has become an end in itself. And while hoarding goes with Silas's "hard isolation," it is really a substitute for the activities upon which the community rests. The guineas provide Silas's "revelry"; he "loved them all"—the coins of all sizes; guineas yet to be earned were like "unborn children"; his piety was the "worship of gold." Here were his play, love, parenthood, religion.

These sharp images are characteristic of the style in the chapters on Silas, where Eliot writes most suggestively and allusively, often figuratively, sometimes symbolically; it is Silas who most stirs her imagination and calls forth a language that keeps our sense of the secondary constantly active. When she describes Silas's class of "pallid undersized men," her words also give us a picture of a pale, restricted life without growth. When Silas, robbed, is compared to "a man falling into dark waters," it is as if a movie camera were switching us for a split second to the literal dark waters into which Dunstan is falling. When she tells us that Silas's "face and figure shrank and bent themselves into a constant mechanical relation to the objects of life," she introduces the theme of the mechanical life which she then develops by various images, for instance, of Silas "deafened and blinded more and more to all things except the monotony of his loom and the repetition of his web." He is variously compared to a spider, to an ant, to an insect, to a "gnome or brownie," as if, though alive, he were less than human. His life is imaged in terms of space: he is shut "close up with his narrow grief," his heart "as a locked casket"; he had "shrunk continually into narrow isolation," into "close-locked solitude," thinking in an "ever-repeated circle," his soul "stupefied in a cold, narrow prison." Silas's life is dark as well as cramped, and the first image of restrictedness is nicely joined with a light image: "The little light he possessed spread its beams so narrowly, that frustrated belief was a curtain broad enough to create for him the blackness of night." The "light of his faith" was "put out." His gold was "hidden away from the daylight"; there was a "dark shadow over the days of his best years."

These constant figures build up a picture of Silas's gold-period as deficient in variety, vitality, spaciousness, illumination. I hope that these examples of Eliot's more packed, suggestive style will tempt other readers to go further in exploring her imaginative resources, for there is plenty of material—the inconspicuous parallels in the action, the ways of presenting Silas's aloofness, the changes in Silas's eyes and sight, the concepts of "mystery" and "dream" that she draws on repeatedly, and the important theme of the hidden life. There is, of course, least indirection and most of the full frontal attack in the chapters on Raveloe life (5, 7, 8, 10, 11). Despite dashes of a fine Austen-like humor that laces these scenes, they are likely to become overextended, and we to dismiss them as the product of a dated unthrifty craftsmanship. Yet this dismissal would be partly wrong, for the village life chapters have a function: they portray the nature of the community from which Silas has been cut off and which he rejoins. Though Eliot interprets this return as a spiritual gain, she will not idealize or sentimentalize community life: so she characterizes it very carefully, at times, I believe, too carefully.

—Robert B. Heilman, "Return to Raveloe: Thirty-five Years After," *English Journal* 46, No. 1 (January 1957), pp. 6–7

A. E. S. VINER ON *SILAS MARNER* AS A REALISTIC FABLE

[A. E. S. Viner is a British literary critic and author of *George Eliot* (1971), from which the following extract is taken. Here, Viner refers to *Silas Marner* as a "realistic fable"—a story full of impossibilities of plot but also of realistic touches in the description of landscape and character.]

The mere skeleton of the plot is filled with impossibilities: Eppie's mother's death just in front of Silas's cottage; Silas's cataleptic attack just at the moment when he was looking out of the door, so that the child entered without his seeing her, etc. The reality lies in the way in which George Eliot has planted the improbabilities of the plot in the firm soil of convincing natural surroundings, so that the reader accepts the coincidences without question. One feels the story's pattern to be expressive of truth in the way that the pattern of one of Aesop's fables, though fantastic and utterly different in tone, may present a profound insight into human behaviour.

The background is built up with deft and telling strokes: for example, the remarkable similarity of education and outlook between the gentry and the peasantry. The squire has the same approach to life as the landlord of the inn, and revealingly, is made to speak a dialect very little more refined. Though Nancy may be the wife of the squire and daughter of the local man of means, she entertains, with no suspicion of demeaning herself, the idea of running her own dairy. But though they may be intellectually on a par, the two classes are completely separate and content to be that way. Even more than in *Adam Bede* (which takes place later in time), the sense of obligation between classes is strongly felt. The few privileged villagers who are allowed to watch the New Year's dancing at the squire's mansion, look on at what is for them a kind of social rite:

> Already Mr. Macey and a few other privileged villagers, who were allowed to be spectators on these great occasions, were seated on benches placed for them near the door; and great was the admiration and satisfaction in that quarter when the couples had formed themselves for the dance, and the Squire led off with Mrs Crackenthorp, joining hands with the Rector and Mrs Osgood. That was as it should be—that was what everybody had been used to—and the charter of Raveloe seemed to be renewed by the ceremony.

Dolly Winthrop, another woman like Mrs Poyser with a gift for racy speech that catches the wisdom and essence of her class, reflects also the degree to which small villages, such as Raveloe, were cut off from the rest of the country in the days before the coming of the railway. She is utterly puzzled by Silas's having gone to "chapel", an institution of which she has never heard: "Dolly was much puzzled at this new word, but she was rather afraid of inquiring further, lest 'chapel' might mean some haunt of wickedness." One of the remarkable aspects of the book is that at no time does George Eliot condescend nor allow the reader to condescend to these humble people. She shows that their attitudes of mind and their moral dilemmas are those which are common to all, regardless of time or education. Though a character may have in a George Eliot novel no comprehension of the most basic of intellectual concepts, his mental processes are ones which we all share, intelligent or stupid, informed or uneducated. ⟨. . .⟩

F. R. Leavis rightly remarks that "There is nothing that strikes us as false about the story; its charm depends upon our being convinced of its moral truth." Ignoring the fact that for this critic charm is a quality not a little suspect, the attribute of "moral truth" is undeniably the one on which the little novel relies most heavily. The story is a fable of re-birth. Silas was a youth of gentle and unquestioning faith, who trusted in his fellow-men; because of these very qualities he is vulnerable. After his false conviction, Silas's faith in his fellow human beings as well as in his religion is shattered, seemingly beyond repair. His former sensitivity makes him a recluse; his affectionate nature makes him a miser—his gold cannot betray him. But gold, though it cannot betray, cannot reciprocate affection. When the child is, as it were, miraculously substituted for the gold, the possibility of reciprocal human feeling, what Wilfred Owen calls "the eternal reciprocity of tears", gradually restores the warmth and faith in his fellows that had lain dormant for so long.

—A. E. S. Viner, *George Eliot* (Edinburgh: Olvier & Boyd, 1971), pp. 58–61

PETER SIMPSON ON THE FOUR PHASES OF SILAS'S HISTORY

[Peter Simpson is a senior lecturer in English at the University of Canterbury in New Zealand. In this extract, Simpson relates the four phases of Silas's life-history to analogous phases in Eliot's own life, while Eppie stands for the "imaginative recovery of childhood in the artist."]

Silas's history falls into four distinct phases which are closely analogous to those which constitute the pattern shared by

Wordsworth and Eliot herself. First, there is Silas's childhood, ending with this conversion to the faith of Lantern Yard; second, the phase of devout piety, ending with his undeserved disgrace and exile and his consequent loss of faith; third, the phase of his 'exile' in Raveloe, his solitary and desolate accumulation of gold through his weaving; this phase ends abruptly with the arrival of Eppie; fourth, the phase of his recovery and his absorption into the community.

The broad parallels between Silas and Eliot are confirmed by a comparison of their ages at the different phases of their lives; there is a remarkably close correlation. There is no evidence in the novel of Silas's age when he experienced conversion, though in George Eliot's case it was when she was fifteen. Her loss of faith came when she was twenty-two; the corresponding event in Silas's life cannot be placed exactly though it was also in his early twenties, since at the time of the theft he is 'not yet forty,' and has been in Raveloe for about fifteen years. George Eliot began writing fiction shortly before her thirty-seventh birthday; she was forty-one when she wrote *Silas Marner*. Silas was also in his late thirties when Eppie came to him. I base this calculation on the fact that in Part II of the novel, sixteen years after the arrival of Eppie, Silas is described as being, 'not more than five-and-fifty.' The close correspondence of these figures confirms the striking similarities in the pattern of the two lives. Both are converted to a variety of fervent evangelical Christianity in adolescence; both in their twenties suffer a grievous shock to their previous beliefs and turn away from their old communities to a new, solitary, and hard-working life; after grinding away for about fifteen years both lives are renovated by a dramatic change, brought about by a child in one case and novels drawing on childhood in the other. Despite the contrast in their outward circumstances their inward lives represent a closely parallel history and metamorphosis.

The crux of my case depends on establishing the symbolic equation of the child Eppie and the imaginative recovery of childhood in the artist; this can only be done by detailed analysis of certain key passages.

The references to Silas's childhood in the novel are few but crucial. The first important thing to note is that Silas is not cut off from his childhood experience by his exile from Lantern Yard. This is in effect a second exile; he has already been deprived of his childhood by his religious fervour:

> He had inherited from his mother some acquaintance with medicinal herbs and their preparation—a little store of wisdom which she had imparted to him as a solemn bequest—but of late years he had had doubts about the lawfulness of applying this knowledge, believing that herbs could have no efficacy without prayer, and that prayer might suffice without herbs; so that his inherited delight to wander through the fields in search of foxglove and dandelion and coltsfoot, began to wear to him the character of a temptation.

It is significant that although Silas's childhood was spent in the city it is always associated in the novel with his memories of wandering through the fields in search of herbs; imaginatively, as it were, Silas had a rural childhood. The contrast between his inherited wisdom of the fields and the world of 'prayer' is emphasized by the fact that the city is always associated with this faith, never with the childhood; thus, his 'narrow religious sect' is identified with the 'little hidden world' of Lantern Yard, 'that obscure religious life which has gone on in the alleys of our towns.'

There is a second significantly placed reference to his childhood shortly after his arrival in Raveloe as if to confirm in this new setting his loss of contact with his earliest experiences. The occasion is Silas's witnessing in one of the villagers the symptoms of the disease that killed his mother:

> He felt a rush of pity at the mingled sight and remembrance, and, recalling the relief his mother had found from a simple preparation of foxglove, he promised Sally Oates to bring her something that would ease her, since the doctor did her no good. In this office of charity, Silas felt, for the first time since he had come to Raveloe, a sense of unity between his past and present life, which might have been the beginning of his rescue from the insect-like existence into which his nature had shrunk.

In this passage the double nature of Silas's isolation is indicated. He is alienated not only from his fellow humans but also from his true self, owing to his severance from his past. Thus his impulse of charity is inseparable from the activation of his memory ("the mingled sight and remembrance'); the 'office of charity' which would tend to break down his social isolation also leads to 'a sense of unity between his past and present life,' that is, the breakdown of his isolation from his true self. Unfortunately, through mutual misunderstanding his charitable impulse ironically 'heightened the repulsion between him and his neighbours, and made his isolation more complete.' The stress Eliot places on the close relationship between the integration of a man with his fellows and the integration of his personality derives as we have seen from her own experience and is central too to Wordsworth's philosophy of 'relationship and love.'

—Peter Simpson, "Crisis and Recovery: Wordsworth, George Eliot, and *Silas Marner*," *University of Toronto Quarterly* 48, No. 2 (Winter 1978–79): 108–10

K. M. Newton on *Silas Marner* and the Organic Society

[K. M. Newton is a professor of English at the University of Dundee in Scotland and the author of *In Defence of Literary Interpretation* (1986), *Interpreting the Text: A Critical Introduction to the Theory and Practice of Literary Interpretation* (1990), and *George Eliot: Romantic Humanist* (1981), from which the following extract is taken. Here, Newton finds in *Silas Marner* an example of an organic society—a society whose moral and cultural values have emerged out of long-standing tradition.]

Raveloe in *Silas Marner* is the clearest example of an organic society in any of George Eliot's works. It is really the community of Raveloe that is the centre of the novel, since it is the acceptance of its way of life, its values and traditions, which cures Silas Marner of the alienation he suffers as a result of the breakdown of the rigid form of Christianity in which he had formerly believed. Raveloe is an example of a pre-industrialised organic community. It has preserved close links with the past, which means that mystery and superstition form part of its way of life. It is not George Eliot's intention to attack such beliefs, though the reader is made aware that some events which seem supernatural to the villagers, like the coming of Eppie into Silas's life, can be accounted for in normal causal terms. In a village like Raveloe, 'where many of the old echoes lingered, undrowned by new voices' (Chapter 1), supernatural explanations are inevitable. Myths and superstitions are the means by which people who live in such communities try to cope with the disorder of experience. Certain past events also take on a mythic function and become dramatisations of the underlying values of the community. The story of the Lammeter's wedding performs such a function. Everyone has heard it many times, but listening to it again creates in people a feeling which reaffirms their community values. It is akin to going to church and attending the New Year dance. These perform the ceremonial function of reinforcing the unity and the implicit values of the community, and are important in giving the people a sense of corporate identity. The individual is able to communicate with others at a deeper level than the merely verbal, since the existence of shared symbols and implicit values creates a deep sense of fellowship. Silas Marner eventually becomes integrated into this society and recovers from his mental crisis. The unified community consciousness is able to provide protection against the amoral otherness which resists human control and categorisation, and which is a potential threat to both the individual and society.

In Raveloe, religion is part of the social fabric and does not require the support of a rigid theology. This is in sharp contrast to industrialised Lantern Yard, where Silas lived originally, in which Christianity has taken the most rigid doctrinal form in the extreme providential beliefs of Silas's sect. People in Raveloe, however, are suspicious of the notion of beneficent providence. Their connection with older, almost pre-Christian traditions prevents such ideas gaining control; as the narrator puts it: 'the rude mind with difficulty associates the ideas of power and benignity' (Chapter 1). Religion, therefore, does not take the extreme forms common in industrialised towns, but the community is nevertheless able to absorb both good and bad fortune. It can accept that the appearance of Eppie apparently in place of Silas's gold has a more than natural meaning, but such a belief does not become hardened into rigid theological form. Raveloe can also accommodate the alternative rational explanation of reality, exemplified by Mr Dowlas in his difference with Mr Macey over whether a ghost or a tramp took Silas's gold. Both of them are wrong, but transcending their differences is the community's awareness of Silas's plight. Though Silas has been a recluse for fifteen years, they are willing to help him, and this, for George Eliot, is more important than differing interpretations of the nature of reality.

George Eliot takes care to portray the atmosphere and feeling of life in Raveloe in the style of the novel by giving the narrative something of the mythic and mysterious qualities of a fairy tale. It is possible that such features were incorporated into the work because she intended that life in Raveloe should serve a kind of mythic function for her own society. By creating the unified social life of Raveloe, she presents the reader with an image that embodies his own need of a similar organic relationship to his own society.

Raveloe is an example of a valuable social form which belongs to the past. George Eliot is not setting it up as a model to be imitated but using it as an example to the present. Carlyle employed a similar tactic in *Past and Present* in his description of an organic feudal society. Raveloe cannot be imitated, but the kind of social and human experience it made possible must be embodied in a new form in the present industrial age. Despite the value of the community life of Raveloe, it is nevertheless clear that it belongs to a time which is passing; the future belongs to industrialised societies like Lantern Yard. There is no going back to that particular form of rural community as a solution to the problems of modern society, but it is implied, I think, that life in an industrialised society needs to be organic in a similar way.

—K. M. Newton, *George Eliot: Romantic Humanist: A Study of the Philosophical Structure of Her Novels* (Basingstoke, UK: Macmillan Press, 1981), pp. 84–86

[Rosemary Ashton (b. 1947) is a professor of English at University College, London. She has written *Little Germany: Exile and Asylum in Victorian England* (1986), The Mill on the Floss: *A Natural History* (1990), and *G. H. Lewes: A Life* (1991). In this extract from *George Eliot* (1983), Ashton examines the influence of William Wordsworth on Eliot.]

The Wordsworthian influence merges, in the simple progress of the plot, with that of Feuerbach's religion of humanity. Silas Marner, the embittered and lonely weaver, loses his gold and finds a golden-haired child, Eppie; the child forces him to forge links with the community and reestablishes his contact with external nature; she 'warmed him into joy because *she* had joy'. Though Silas has lost his religious belief, he submits to the dominant religion of Raveloe—a mixture of primitive superstition and kind practical wisdom—for the child's sake. He has her baptised to please his neighbours and to 'do the right thing'. The significance of the event is not, however, primarily religious, but human: by it Silas shares in the human fellowship of the community. George Eliot's treatment is unusually optimistic:

> In old days there were angels who came and took men by the hand and led them away from the city of destruction. We see no white-winged angels now. But yet men are led away from threatening destruction: a hand is put into theirs, which leads them forth gently towards a calm and bright land, so that they look no more backward; and the hand may be a little child's.

The fact that no agent is assigned to the action of leading men away from destruction suggests that the optimism is rather forced, being a necessary part of George Eliot's mild, Wordsworthian plan (in which a benevolent external Nature may be the agent of human regeneration), rather than fully endorsed by her.

The nemesis to which she refers in her letter to Blackwood is that which befalls Godfrey Cass, son of the squire, who by secretly marrying a girl beneath him in rank has sown the seed which 'by orderly sequence brings forth a seed after its kind'. Eppie is Godfrey's child by his imprudent marriage; he takes care not to own up to the relationship, thus clearing a path towards possible marriage with Nancy Lammeter, but also denying himself the opportunity of rearing and loving Eppie. Godfrey's 'moral cowardice' is deftly sketched early in the novel:

> The results of confession were not contingent, they were certain; whereas betrayal was not certain. From the near vision of that certainty he fell back on suspense and vacillation with a sense of repose. The disinherited son of a small squire, equally disinclined to dig and to beg, was almost as helpless as an uprooted tree, which, by the favour of earth and sky, has grown to a handsome bulk on the spot where it first shot upward. . . . he would rather trust to casualties than to his own resolve—rather go on sitting at the feast and sipping the wine he loved, though with the sword hanging over him and terror in his heart, than rush away into the cold darkness where there was no pleasure left.

Godfrey's 'god'—'Favourable Chance'—appears to smile on him: the abandoned opium-addicted wife dies. But Godfrey's relief at not being found out becomes saddened as the years pass and he watches his daughter Eppie grow up happy with her adopted father, while his marriage with Nancy produces no children. Nemesis, gold-symbolism and plot proceed in step, so that just when Silas's gold is found, he is threatened with the corresponding loss of golden-haired Eppie. But the tale is 'regenerative'. Eppie's true affections are for Silas, and she refuses to be adopted by Godfrey. It is a neat, rather uncharacteristic work by George Eliot, except in the link between character and action, and in the idea of the nemesis of conscience which she sketches here in Godfrey Cass.

—Rosemary Ashton, *George Eliot* (New York: Oxford University Press, 1983), pp. 48–49

SANDRA M. GILBERT ON EPPIE

[Sandra M. Gilbert (b. 1936), a professor of English at the University of California at Davis, has cowritten (with Susan Gubar) a history of women's writing in the nine-

teenth century, *The Madwoman in the Attic* (1979), followed by a three-volume study of women's writing in
this century, *No Man's Land* (1988–94). In this extract,
Gilbert discusses the role of Eppie, whose function
seems to reside in being subservient to Silas, the
father-figure.]

Certainly Eliot had long been concerned with the social significance and cultural possibilities of daughterhood. Both *The Mill
on the Floss*—the novel that precedes *Silas Marner*—and
Romola—the one that follows it—are elaborate examinations
of the structural inadequacies of a daughter's estate. As for
Marian Evans, moreover, her real life had persistently confronted her with the problematic nature of daughterhood and its
corollary condition, sisterhood. As biographers have shown,
her feelings for her own father were ambivalent not only during
his lifetime but throughout hers; yet his superegoistic legacy
pervaded other relationships she formed. When she was in her
early twenties, for instance, she became a dutiful disciple to the
Casaubon-like Dr. Brabant, who "punningly baptized her
Deutera because she was to be a second daughter to him."
And even when she was a middle-aged woman, she remembered her older brother Isaac as a kind of miniature father, "a
Like unlike, a Self that self restrains," observing wistfully that
"were another childhood-world my share, / I would be born a
little sister there." Since "Eppie" was the name of Silas' little
sister, it seems likely that, in being "born" again to the mild
weaver, Marian Evans did in fiction if not in fact re-create herself as both daughter and little sister.

Certainly Eppie's protestations of daughterly devotion suggest that she is in some sense a born-again daughter. "I should
have no delight i' life any more if I was forced to go away from
my father," she tells Nancy and Godfrey Cass. Like the Marian
Evans who became "Deutera," Eppie is not so much a second
daughter as twice a daughter—a double daughterly daughter.
As such a "Deutera," she is the golden girl whose being reiterates those cultural commandments Moses set forth for the second time in Deuteronomy. Thus, although scrupulous Nancy
Lammeter Cass has often been seen as articulating Eliot's moral
position on the key events of this novel, it is really the more
impulsive Eppie who is the conscience of the book.

This becomes clearest when Nancy argues that "there's a duty you owe to your lawful father." Eppie's instant reply, with its counterclaim that "I can't feel as I've got any father but one," expresses a more accurate understanding of the idea of fatherhood. For in repudiating *God-free* Cass, who is only by chance (*casus*) her natural father, and affirming Silas Marner, who is by choice her cultural father, Eppie rejects the lawless father in favor of the lawful one, indicating her clear awareness that fatherhood itself is both *a* social construct (or, in Stephen Dedalus' words, "a legal fiction") and *the* social construct that constructs society. Having achieved and acted on this analysis, she is rewarded with a domestic happiness which seems to prove Dickinson's contention that it is "vain to punish Honey, / It only sweeter grows." At the same time, in speaking such a law, this creature of milk and honey initiates the reeducation and redemption of Godfrey Cass: the cultural code of Deuteronomy speaks through her, suggesting that, even if she is a Christmas child, she is as much a daughter of the Old Testament as of the New, of the first telling of the law as of its second telling.

Happy and dutiful as she is, however, Eppie is not perfectly contented, for she has a small fund of anxiety that is pledged to her other parent—her lost mother. This intermittent sadness, which manifests itself as a preoccupation with her mother's wedding ring, directs our attention to a strange disruption at the center of *Silas Marner:* the history of Eppie's dead mother. On the surface, of course, the ring that Silas has saved for his adopted daughter is an aptly ironic symbol of that repressed plot, since there never was any bond beyond an artificial one between Molly Farren and Godfrey Cass, the lawless father "of whom [the ring] was the symbol." But Eppie's frequent ruminations on the questions of "how her mother looked, whom she was like, and how [Silas] had found her against the furze bush" suggest that there is something more problematic than a traditional bad marriage at issue here. As so often in this "legendary tale," what seems like a moral point also offers an eerily accurate account of what Freud sees as the inexorable psychosexual growth and entry of the daughter into a culture shaped by the codes of the father. "Our insight into [the pre-Oedipus] phase in the little girl's development comes to us as a surprise, comparable . . . with . . . the discovery of the Minoan-Mycenaean civilization behind that of Greece," remarks Freud, explaining that "everything connected with this first mother-attachment has . . . seemed to me . . . lost in a past so dim and shadowy . . . that it seemed as if it had undergone some specially inexorable repression."

Indeed, Molly Farren *has* undergone a "specially inexorable repression" in this novel. Three or four pages of a single chapter are devoted to her, though her damned and doomed wanderings in the snow strikingly recapitulate the lengthier wanderings of fallen women like Hetty Sorel and Maggie Tulliver. I suggest that Eliot attempts this drastic condensation precisely because *Silas Marner,* in allowing her to speak symbolically about the meaning of daughterhood, also allowed her to speak in even more resonant symbols about the significance of motherhood. What she said was what she saw: that it is better to be a daughter than a mother and better still to be a father than a daughter. For when the Deuteronomy of culture formulates the incest laws that lie at the center of human society, that severe code tells the son: "You may not have your mother; you may not kill your father." But when it is translated into a "Daughteronomy" preached for the growing girl, it says: "You must bury your mother; you must give yourself to your father." Since the daughter has inherited an empty pack and cannot *be* a father, she has no choice but to be *for* the father—to be his treasure, his land, his voice.

—Sandra M. Gilbert, "Life's Empty Pack: Notes toward a Literary Daughteronomy," *Critical Inquiry* 11, No. 3 (March 1985): 362–64

GILLIAN BEER ON MAGIC AS TRANSCENDENT NATURE

[Gillian Beer (b. 1935) is a professor of English at Cambridge University and the author of *Meredith: A Change of Masks* (1970) and *Darwin's Plots: Evolutionary Narrative in Darwin, George Eliot, and Nineteenth*

Century Fiction (1983). In this extract from *George Eliot* (1986), Beer argues that *Silas Marner* "proves that 'magic is transcendent nature.' "]

Silas Marner, the work which interrupted and delayed *Romola*, is George Eliot's story which proves that 'magic is transcendent nature'. The folk-tale mode of the opening, the ballad-like elements in the story of Godfrey Cass and his secret marriage to opium addict Molly, Silas's uncanny trances, the mythic substitution of child for gold in a healing inversion of the Midas myth (where Midas unwittingly turns his little daughter into a gold statue): all these elements declare the extent to which the work draws on fairy-tale to sustain its transformations.

The figure of Silas, bent and isolated, has overtones of Rumpelstiltskin, another male weaver with a penchant for babies. But these allusions (Midas, Rumpelstiltskin, the Norns), are all there to be lost and obliterated. They are part of the system of expectation and allusion which we must respond to, and dispel, if we are to reach the human directness of the work. The manifest is here, peculiarly, the meaning. Silas is not feminised; he is not a woman. He is a man, a celibate, who nurtures a girl-child and thus becomes her father. As she wrote, George Eliot seems to have determined to demonstrate how far transformation is a human power, and in the figure of Silas she sets out to show how not only his, but his society's assumptions, are changed.

Silas is a weaver, deliberately set *across* the stereotype of the woman weaving, which, though it may have derived from social practice in ancient Greece, certainly did not correspond to conditions after the onset of the industrial revolution in England. 'The Fates at their weaving' was a familiar literary trope, but home-weaving was already largely a thing of the past at the time George Eliot wrote and was no longer a woman's occupation.

Silas Marner humanises George Eliot's increasing fascination with the action of chance. This fascination was intellectually reinforced by Darwin's insistence on 'chance' mutation as happening to fit or unfit an organism for its medium, but it was also forced on her by her practice as a novelist. In an excellent analysis George Levine (1962) has analyzed the function of determinism in George Eliot's work; but we are equally made aware of coincidence, of the haphazard assemblage of circumstances by which things come to be. The process can be most acutely observed where there is a secret to be kept. As the narrative comments in *The Mill on the Floss*:

> Secrets are rarely betrayed or discovered according to any programme our fear has sketched out. Fear is almost always haunted by terrible dramatic scenes, which recur in spite of the best-argued probabilities against them. . . . Those slight indirect suggestions which are dependent on apparently trivial coincidences and incalculable states of mind, are the favourite machinery of Fact, but are not the stuff in which imagination is apt to work.

This commentary describes a technical problem for the novelist: the reader may more readily be reconciled to dream-scenes of discovery and confrontation than to the minute operations of the trivial and incalculable. We have already seen in 'The Lifted Veil' that George Eliot was as much aware of the factitiousness of concealing the contrivances in a narrative as of the disruptiveness of laying them open. The writer makes choices. Does that make her also responsible for the events of the work? Must she become the book's 'transcendental signifier', occupying the place of God the Father? Since, outside the fiction, George Eliot rejected the figure of God and was declaredly against any belief in personal providence and personal afterlife, this technical problem was one she shared at the opposite end of the spectrum with Muriel Spark. Spark delights in manifesting chance, plot, contrivance, as a representation of divine plotting, a plot inscrutable and uncomfortable but unavoidably in charge. Ideologically, George Eliot needed to find a quite other organisation for plot. She needed one which would allow sufficient capaciousness for coincidence to issue from the largesse of possibility without any implication of plan. This was the method she took to its fullest extent in *Middlemarch*, but even there she found it necessary to turn to law as narrative metaphor. Law, and lawyers' confidentiality and strategy, could figure the ineluctable connections of unlike which manifest themselves as coincidence.

—Gillian Beer, *George Eliot* (Bloomington: Indiana University Press, 1986), pp. 125–28

[Sally Shuttleworth (b. 1952) is the author of *George Eliot and Nineteenth Century Science* (1984), the editor of Eliot's *The Mill on the Floss* (1991), and the coeditor of *Nature Transformed: Science and Literature 1700–1900* (1989). In this extract, Shuttleworth finds a scientific underpinning to the fairy-tale quality of *Silas Marner* in its equation of the physical isolation of Silas Marner from his community and his emotional isolation.]

Physiological psychology allows George Eliot to explore the disjunction between Silas's experience and that of the surrounding village life. The physical terms in fact reinforce the moral point of his social isolation. Ultimately, however, George Eliot employs the unified vocabulary of social and psychological analysis to reaffirm the ideals of organic continuity. Though Silas's social experience has been that of disruption, discontinuity and growing isolation, his life is radically transformed by the sudden appearance of the child Eppie, who stimulates forgotten channels of his mind, thus operating as a catalyst to release his energy. Eliot is careful to make Silas's first response one of memory:

> Could this be his little sister come back to him in a dream . . .?
> . . . It was very much like his little sister. Silas sank into his chair powerless, under the double presence of an inexplicable surprise and a hurrying influx of memories. (Ch. XII)

This crucial analysis is based upon physiological principles of directed force. It conforms both to Lewes's conception of the mind as an 'aggregate of forces' and to his theories of unconscious association. The sight of the child stimulates 'a vision of the old home and the old streets leading to Lantern Yard—and within that vision another, of the thoughts which had been present with him in those far-off scenes' (ch. XII). Silas's sequence of memory illustrates the 'law of attraction' defined here by Spencer: 'that when any two psychical states occur in immediate succession, an effect is produced such that if the first subsequently recurs there is a certain tendency for the second to follow.' The physical processes of unconscious association establish continuity in personal life, a continuity which Spencer believed was then passed on to future generations through the physiological inheritance of 'modified nervous tendencies.' Spencer's theories of progressive social evolution were in fact founded on the premise that unconscious association formed the basis of the individual's adaptation to the environment, and thence of the race's progressive development as these 'forms of thought' were transmitted to offspring. Since relations to the environment, once established, are, he argues, 'uniform, invariable, incapable of being absent, or reversed, or abolished, they must be represented by irreversible, indestructible connections of ideas.' The physiological unity of mind is taken as a guarantee of essential social continuity and development.

Though George Eliot does not share Spencer's ebullient optimism, it is undoubtedly the physiological unity of Silas's mind, represented by his unconscious association of ideas, that allows him to heal the breach in his social experience, to grow once more into union with his neighbours, and into a sense of continuity with his past. Eppie's gradual progressive development is mirrored in Silas as the underlying continuity of his past. Eppie's gradual progressive development is mirrored in Silas as the underlying continuity of his history is revealed:

> As the child's mind was growing into knowledge, his mind was growing into memory: as her life unfolded, his soul, long stupefied in a cold narrow prison, was unfolding too, and trembling gradually into full consciousness. (Ch. XIV)

The term 'full consciousness' is here replete with meaning: it implies not only an integrated sense of self based on continuous memory, but also an open, accepting awareness of surrounding social life. Under the influence of Eppie, Silas moves beyond the 'ever-repeated circle' of thought established by his gold to look for links and ties with his neighbours. He learns to channel his previously inert feelings into 'the forms of custom and belief which were the mould of Raveloe life; and as, with reawakening sensibilities, memory also reawakened, he had begun to ponder over the elements of his old faith, and blend them with his new impressions, till he recovered a consciousness of unity between his past and present' (ch. XVI). Social isolation and personal disruption are replaced by integration.

Silas's change appears a dramatic transformation. In an unexpected reversal, he acquires both a coherent identity and membership of the social community. George Eliot carefully ensures, however, that his development does not violate uniformitarian principles. Eppie's appearance does not radically alter Silas's psychic make-up, it merely reawakens dormant fibres. Though Eppie is compared to the angels who led men away from the city of destruction (ch. XIV), there are no miracles involved in Silas's restoration: the natural chain of causation is not broken. As Strauss argued in his *Life of Jesus*, 'no just notion of the true nature of history is possible without a perception of the inviolability of the chain of finite causes, and of the impossibility of miracles.' Where the scientific principles of physiological psychology had earlier underpinned the analysis of Silas's alienation, they now endorse his growth into unity. His change confirms the principles of organic social evolution. Apparent discontinuity is discounted by the stable physiological structure of his mind. History, as the moral critique of Godfrey implied, is cumulative.

—Sally Shuttleworth, "Fairy Tale or Science? Physiological Psychology in *Silas Marner*," *Languages of Nature: Critical Essays on Science and Literature*, ed. L. J. Jordanova (New Brunswick, NJ: Rutgers University Press, 1986), pp. 279–81

KERRY MCSWEENEY ON SOME FLAWS IN *SILAS MARNER*

[Kerry McSweeney (b. 1941) is the Molson Professor of English at McGill University in Montreal, Canada. He has written critical studies of *Middlemarch* (1984), Ralph Ellison's *Invisible Man* (1988), and *George Eliot: A Literary Life* (1991), from which the following extract is taken. Here, McSweeney finds fault with chapter eighteen of *Silas Marner*.]

If there is a serious flaw in the execution of *Silas Marner*, it occurs in chapter 18—the brief perfunctory scene in which

Godfrey finally tells his wife Nancy what he has long failed to muster the courage to say: that he is the father of Eppie, the child whom sixteen years before Silas took for his own while he remained silent. Earlier in the novel the twistings of Godfrey's conscience and the pattern of his habitual indecision had been detailed; and the previous chapter had offered an extended inside view of Nancy that summarised her fifteen years of marriage, registered her perception that the lack of children was the one privation to which her husband could not be reconciled, and finely analysed the code of conduct and processes of thought that had led her to the view that adoption of children was against the will of Providence. But in chapter 18 no inside view is offered of either husband or wife. One learns nothing about the psychological circumstances that have led Godfrey to break his long silence, nor about any apprehensions he might have had concerning his wife's reaction. And Nancy's response to the news is registered solely through external notation. There is not a scintilla of information concerning her response to the revelation that her husband had been previously married and had fathered a child.

One suspects that the reason for the perfunctoriness of this chapter is a combination of authorial impatience to get to the climactic confrontation scene between the two fathers and the calculation that a fuller treatment of the Godfrey-Nancy interaction would have led to an imbalance in the plots. Whatever the reasons, chapter 19 is all that it should be and contains, *inter alia*, an acuity of psychological notation concerning Godfrey and Nancy that does much to compensate for its absence in the previous chapter. In this splendid scene Godfrey's nemesis— Eppie's refusal to change her station in life—is shown to be deserved not only because of his past irresolution and dependence on chance but also because of a certain spot of commonness (to borrow a phrase from *Middlemarch*) linked to his privileged social position. In thinking that he has a right to Eppie, whose presence in his life would make his married happiness complete, Godfrey betrays a degree of unreflecting egotism not untypical of the way it is 'with all men and woman who reach middle age without the clear perception that life never *can* be thoroughly joyous: under the vague dulness of the grey hours, dissatisfaction seeks a definite object, and finds it in the privation of an untried good' (ch. 17).

Husband and wife explain that they intend to make a lady of Eppie (it is what Hetty Sorrell hoped that Arthur Donnithorne would do for her). When Eppie replies that she can't leave her father and couldn't give up 'the folks I've been used to', Godfrey feels an irritation made inevitable by his inability 'to enter with lively appreciation into other people's feelings'; and his utterance is not unmixed with anger when he urges his 'natural claim . . . that must stand before every other'. Even Nancy shows a similar spot of commonness connected with her 'plenteous circumstances and the privileges of "respectability'". Despite the 'acute sensibility of her own affections', her sympathies are insufficiently extended to enable her to enter 'into the pleasures which early nurture and habit connect with all the little aims and efforts of the poor who are born poor'.

While the two plots of which *Silas Marner* is composed are roughly equal quantitatively, it is the Marner plot that is qualitatively superior. The key to the distinction of this half of the novel is found in extensive use of psychological omniscience on what would seem to be a most unpromising subject—an unlettered linen weaver of pinched background and narrow notions whose consciousness has been further shrivelled as a result of betrayal and subsequent estrangement from human or natural comforters. The decision to apply the fullness of narratorial omniscience to this subject was the key creative decision taken by Marian Evans. In her February 1861 letter to her publisher explaining her intention (setting 'in a strong light the remedial influences of pure, natural human relations'), she observed that 'since William Wordsworth is dead', she could imagine that few would be interested in such an endeavour. Presumably with Wordsworthian precedents in mind, she had felt that her subject—the linen weaver remembered from childhood that had come to her 'as a sort of legendary tale'— 'would have lent itself best to metrical rather than prose fiction'. But as her mind dwelt upon the subject, she became 'inclined to a more realistic treatment'.

—Kerry McSweeney, *George Eliot: A Literary Life* (New York: St. Martin's Press, 1991), pp. 75–77

[Nancy L. Paxton (b. 1949) is a professor of English at Northern Arizona University and the author of *George Eliot and Herbert Spencer* (1991), from which the following extract is taken. Here, Paxton finds in *Silas Marner* a searching discussion of the male psychology of love and fatherhood.]

In *Silas Marner,* Eliot focuses attention on the male psychology of love and attachment by contrasting Silas's regeneration through the recovery of the maternal in himself with the repression of parental feelings that prevents Godfrey's similar redemption and integration. Though he feels some guilt in denying his tie to both Molly Cass and his daughter, Godfrey does not confess the secret of his past marriage and his relation to Eppie until after he witnesses a clear showing of the power of Nemesis in his life. When the waters at the Stone-pits recede, they expose Dunstan's skeleton and Silas's gold, and suggest, by their juxtaposition, the killing power of the obsession with money that destroys brotherly love. Godfrey is not himself immune from this obsession, for when he arrives at Silas's cottage sixteen years after he renounced his daughter, he approaches the disclosure of his paternity awkwardly, though not coincidentally, by talking about the recovery of Silas's gold and hinting that it might not be sufficient to meet his needs in old age.

In the exchange between Godfrey and Silas, which enunciates two differing views of fatherhood, Eliot demonstrates how Godfrey's assumptions based on the "natural" law of biological paternity are defeated by Silas's appeals to a "moral" law that transcends it. Godfrey's rhetoric shows that he still views Eppie as a possession that could be exchanged for money. He begins with an economic argument that seems to him to be the most obvious and persuasive one to convince Silas to surrender Eppie: he asks if Silas wouldn't "like to see her taken care of by those who can leave her well off and make a lady of her" and promises him "every reward" as a compensation (ch. 19). Godrey's embarrassed assertion of his "preeminent" and "natural claim" on Eppie shows that his first impulse is to use the economic metaphors which associate fatherhood with possession, metaphors Spencer unself-consciously employs in his analysis of erotic and parental love in *The Principles of Psychology*.

When Godfrey fails to claim Eppie by this "natural" right of the father, he resorts to an assertion of his patriarchal authority as chief lawgiver in Raveloe. Reminding Silas of his daughter's permanent minority under the law, Godfrey again addresses himself to Silas: "You ought to remember your own life's uncertain, and she's at an age now when her lot may soon be fixed in a way different from what it would be in her father's home; she may marry some low working man, and then, whatever I might do, I couldn't make her well off" (ch. 19). Godfrey's very bluntness discloses the stark reality of the social compact between fathers and daughters in Eppie's world—and in Eliot's own—where married women were still denied the right to claim their own wages or to own property. In resorting to such economic and legal arguments, Godfrey reveals an understanding of kinship that attends to the letter rather than the spirit of the law, a perspective that is evident in Spencer's brief discussion of marriage and fatherhood in *The Principles of Psychology*.

Eliot counters this traditional view of fatherhood by asserting an alternative interpretation, and investing not only Silas but Eppie with some of the epic authority she gave to Maggie Tulliver in *The Mill on the Floss*. Though Silas appeals to a superior Divine Authority in resisting Godfrey's offers, he ultimately refuses to speak for Eppie. Silas identifies a moral authority that supersedes natural and civil law in Eppie's case: "God gave her to me because you turned your back upon her, and he looks upon her as mine; you've no right to her! When a man turns a blessing from his door, it falls to them as take it in" (ch. 19). In spite of his desperate desire to "keep her," though, Silas submits himself finally to Eppie's will, saying, "Eppie, my child speak. I won't stand in your way" (ch. 19), and later reminds Godfrey that he will not bargain with him for the child he loves (ch 19). In this way, Silas shows that he has freed himself from the delusion that originally prompted him to confuse the foundling on his hearth with his lost gold; Godfrey, in contrast, remains imprisoned by similar economic metaphors until he is forced to see beyond them when his daughter repudiates his claims.

Eliot is quite explicit about Eppie's refusal to surrender herself to the traditional compact which allows the father to transform the daughter into a "treasure" to be exchanged in marriage. Eppie feels her heart swell in sympathy at Silas's sudden understanding of Godfrey's intention to separate him from the child he has loved with "perfect love" (ch. 16), but her choice to stand loyally by him is not a blind act of filial obedience but rather an expression of her capacity to "judge" and speak for herself. When Godfrey describes all the fine things he would give her in exchange if she would come to live at Red House, Eppie sees his offer as a bribe and feels a "repulsion toward the offered lot and the newly revealed father" (ch. 19). She says, "It'd be poor work for me to put on things, and ride in a gig, and sit in a place at church, as 'ud make them as I'm fond of think me unfitting company for 'em" (ch. 19).

In emphasizing those capacities for language and love that separate humans from other animals, Eliot thus registers her disagreement with Spencer, who focused primarily on mankind's economic and productive capacities. Silas counters Godfrey's appeal, by saying: "Your coming now and saying 'I'm her father' doesn't alter the feeling inside us. It's me she's been calling her father ever since she could say the word" (ch. 19). Eppie's feelings likewise "vibrate" to "every word" Silas speaks, and so she rejects Godfrey's offer and acts instead on her profound sympathy for the man who has "loved her from the first," and has played the part of both mother and father in her life. Thus, Eppie transcends the word of law as it is patriarchally defined and asserts instead her own right to the power of naming, when she says, "I can't feel as I've got any father but one" (ch. 19). Her words, and later her appropriation of her right to name her own desire to marry Aaron Winthrop, make Godfrey realize, finally, that "there's debts we can't pay like money debts" (ch. 20).

Nancy L. Paxton, *George Eliot and Herbert Spencer: Feminism, Evolutionism, and the Reconstruction of Gender* (Princeton: Princeton University Press, 1991), pp. 110–12

[Kristin Brady (b. 1949) is a professor of English at the University of Western Ontario in Canada. She has written *The Short Stories of Thomas Hardy* (1982) and *George Eliot* (1992), from which the following extract is taken. Here, Brady argues that the presence of Molly Cass disrupts the sense of closure at the end of *Silas Marner*.]

The powerful but problematic presence of Molly Cass in *Silas Marner* disrupts even the novel's ostensibly satisfying closure, in which Eppie rejects her biological father while favouring the adoptive parent and completes the family circle by marrying a man who will play the role of son to Silas Marner (forebodingly anticipating Romola's destructive marriage). All of the characters who have borne a significant relationship to Eppie are somehow present at her marriage: Marner plays the parental role he deserves and Dolly occupies the double place of godmother and mother of the groom, while Nancy and Godfrey Cass—though absent—supply the wedding dress and party. Only Molly's implied presence in the novel's closure is ignored by the narrator, who in ending the story describes the garden at Stone-pits, where 'the flowers shone with answering gladness, as the four united people came within sight of them'. What is left unmentioned here, significantly, is that the garden which stands as an image of this new union contains the furze-bush (conventionally associated with the fallen woman) on which Molly's corpse was found, which Eppie had transplanted in her mother's memory. Molly Cass's death—the event which had made possible the happiness of the wedding party—is thus subliminally present in the novel's ending and, in spite of the narrator's failure to mention it, stands as a reminder of the loss that has accomplished the happy closure.

Nor is the seeming symmetry of the "four united people' without its nagging loose ends. Marner and Dolly, for example, can appear as a couple here only because Winthrop has just "found it agreeable to turn in' at the Rainbow rather than going back to the house with his family (Conclusion). Nor is the marriage of Aaron and Eppie necessarily an image of perfect harmony. Though the relationship is generally presented in the idealised terms of fairy tale, the narrator has offered one hint of Eppie's frustrated desire for knowledge and power. When Marner proposes the visit to Lantern Yard, Eppie is

> very joyful, for there was the prospect not only of wonder and delight at seeing a strange country, but also of coming back to tell Aaron all about it. Aaron was so much wiser than she was about most things—it would be rather pleasant to have this little advantage over him.

Even in the overdetermined happy closure of Eliot's most fable-like novel are veiled references to a suppression of women that is necessary for the construction of happy patriarchal families. By definition, the romance plot requires that the fulfilment of Marner and Aaron be more complete than that of Dolly and Eppie. Behind this asymmetrical closure, moreover, stands the plot whose own closure has enabled the resolution of the romance plot. Like Lucy and Hetty, Molly—Eliot's only married fallen woman and another lost mother—must die before the patriarchal family can achieve its happy consummation.

—Kristin Brady, *George Eliot* (New York: St. Martin's Press, 1992), pp. 117–18

PATRICK SWINDEN ON THE VIRTUES OF *SILAS MARNER*

[Patrick Swinden (b. 1941) is lecturer in English language and literature at the University of Manchester in England. He is the author of *Unofficial Selves: Characters in the Novel from Dickens to the Present Day* (1973) and *Paul Scott: Images of India* (1980). In this extract from his study of *Silas Marner* (1992), Swinden notes that the novel generally avoids two flaws that mar Eliot's other works—excessive "high-

"high-mindedness" and sentimental attachment to a
particular character.]

For most of its length, *Silas Marner* is the most nearly perfect
piece of writing George Eliot ever accomplished. The story of
Silas's expulsion from the religious community of Lantern Yard,
of his arrival at Raveloe and his accumulation there of his hoard
of golden guineas, of the relationships of Godfrey and Dunstan
Cass with the Squire, of Dunsey's theft of the guineas, and of
the events occurring during the New Year's Eve dance at the
Red House is consummately dealt with. The immediate consequences of the discovery of Molly Farren's body and of the
baby are also convincingly described. The events of 16 years
later, briefly related in Part 2, are less well handled; but this is a
short section of seven, for the most part brief, chapters, and the
main issue of the delayed judgment on Godfrey Cass and,
indirectly, on his wife Nancy, is skillfully managed. None of
George Eliot's other works of fiction is as good all the way
through. Those sturdy narratives of guilt and repentance are
always in danger of being undermined by a vein of unlovely
high-mindedness or by lapses of control issuing from the
author's sentimental self-identification with one or other of the
dramatis personae.

The high-mindedness is everywhere apparent in George
Eliot, but it is often matched by a subject seen to be genuinely
worthy of it. Where this is the case there can be no objection.
But sometimes the sense of worth is more apparent than real,
and the presence of, say, Philip Wakem in *The Mill on the Floss*
or of Will Ladislaw in *Middlemarch* goes some distance toward
weakening what are otherwise in most respects admirable novels. Elsewhere the presence of these plaster saints is compre-
hensively baleful. The exhalation of old cassocks and the whiff
of incense that attends them makes these characters unsympa-
thetic to all but the most ardent of George Eliot's devotees. In
his review of John Cross's *Life of George Eliot*, Henry James
describes the Priory, where she lived from 1863 to 1880, as a
"sequestered precinct." He could remember well "a kind of
sanctity in the place, an atmosphere of stillness and concentra-
tion, something that suggested a literary temple." The few pictures of George Eliot that have come down to us are almost all
pictures of the author of characters who might well be imag-

ined as issuing from such a place. It is not a happy thought to be confronted by the subject of Sir Frederic Burton's chalk drawing of 1865, though it has to be added that such was that subject's personal magnetism that many of her contemporaries were happy to be so confronted. In later life she was herself made into the object of just such admiration as she had lavished on Romola and Deronda, with equally appalling results for her posthumous reputation. This did not recover until well into the present century (she died in 1880). For this reason I have chosen for the frontispiece of this book a less familiar chalk drawing by Samuel Laurence, which also has the attraction of having been sketched in 1860, at a date very close to that of the composition of *Silas Marner.*

The other fault, of indulgent self-identification with her characters, is present throughout the novels, but especially in the portrait of Maggie Tulliver in *The Mill on the Floss* and of Dorothea Brooke in *Middlemarch.* George Eliot's handling of these characters has been the subject of prolonged controversy in recent years, and there is no doubt that her perception of some of their faults is as intelligent as her emotional inclination to pardon them is overwhelming. But the one tends to be compromised by the other, and as a result there is something fundamentally unsatisfactory in the way these centrally placed characters are presented to the reader. There is a tendency for the focus to blur at crucial stages in the description of their moral development, and when this happens the picture we get of them looks uncannily like that glazed sympathetic smile emerging from the chalk marks of Sir Frederic's portrait.

The good negative thing that can be said of *Silas Marner* is that until Eppie grows up, three quarters of the way through it, none of these faults appears. There are no plaster saints, and there are no St. Theresas of Arbury Hall Farm on display. But there is plenty of evidence of more positive aspects of George Eliot's personality and genius, which, on the basis of a reading of the other novels, one might have thought were inextricably bound up with these faults. There is a sympathetic understanding of human weakness that too often seems inseparable from certain habits of condescension and moral uplift in her earlier novels. There is a calm contemplation of the inevitable consequences of moral slackness and thoughtless self-indulgence, but without the smug "I told you so's" tagged on at the end of them. And there is a scrupulous attention to the minutiae of motive, the subtle shifts of deception and self-deception, which complicate our responses to her characters' lives. In addition there is her unspectacular and utterly convincing representation of ordinary life bumping along from day to day and from season to season, in the provincial circumstances of her cast of English Midland village characters. No one has done this better than George Eliot does it here.

This is not to say that George Eliot does not reveal herself as a moralist in *Silas Marner*. She does make moral judgments, which do issue from analyses of the minds and motives of her characters. But she does not confuse the morally charged and the morally neutral aspects of her story. This combination of moral passion and curiosity about both the interior and exterior lives of her characters is what makes *Silas Marner* still worth reading, in such changed historical circumstances as today's.

—Patrick Swinden, Silas Marner: *Memory and Salvation* (New York: Twayne, 1992), pp. 9–11

ALAN W. BELLRINGER ON CHARACTER DELINEATION AND TONE IN *SILAS MARNER*

[Alan W. Bellringer is the author of a critical study of Henry James's *The Ambassadors* (1984) as well as monographs on Henry James (1988) and George Eliot (1993), from which the following extract is taken. Here, Bellringer comments on the frequently satirical tone used by Eliot to depict character and to make known her views on social class.]

Though the story of *Silas Marner* encompasses both pathos and sentiment, the tone can be unsparing when it comes to the faults of our 'rural forefathers', those flushed and dull-eyed people without the "higher sensibility that accompanies higher culture' (Ch. 13). There is a radical undertone in the presentation of the squirearchy and the backward pre-industrial village which brings the story closer to Crabbe than to George Eliot's favourite Goldsmith. Henry James's admiration for the display of the 'grossly material life of agriculture England' in the days of 'full-orbed Toryism' in *Silas Marner* is justified. Even Dolly Winthrop, with her refusal to 'speak ill o' this world' in case she offends the powers above, lets slip that 'if there is any good to be got, we've need on it i' this world—that we have' and adds 'what wi' the drink, and the quarrelling, and the bad illnesses, and the hard dying, as I've seen times and times, one's thankful to hear of a better' (Ch. 10). The story cannot, therefore, be truly said to be 'comfortably' set among squires and weavers in the 'rich central plain' of England; it is set rather in 'what we are pleased to call Merry England' (Ch. 1), and that includes places characterised by inefficient farming and social immobility.

The exercise of authority based on land-ownership is noted with much harsher sarcasm in *Silas Marner* than in *Adam Bede*. The whole Cass family is sharply portrayed. The men's weaknesses are traced in an inner and outer cause, the lack of a presiding female presence at the Red House and their unchallenged assumption of superiority, with resulting casualness, indecisiveness and treachery. The New Year dance scene brings a shift of perspective. It is the first scene presented through a female consciousness, that of Nancy Lammeter. We are drawn to Nancy through her concern for her less pretty sister and through the malice of the two town-bred Miss Gunns, who regard her dialectal speech as vulgar and her dispensing with servants as a form of ignorance. When the narrator tell us that Nancy 'had the essential attributes of a lady, high veracity, delicate honour in her dealings, deference to others, and refined personal habits' (Ch. 11), she is successfully protecting the character's virtue against snobbery, that of the Miss Gunns. But Godfrey Cass cannot be protected from the snobbery to which he himself contributes. The class barrier thus erected proves too high for Godfrey to cross at the end. Yet the 'hereditary ease and dignity' of the Cass family is for Godfrey 'a sort of reason for living' (Ch. 3); and Dunsey Cass, whose dull mind is stimulated only by cupidity, is still to be thought of as a 'young gentleman', to whom walking is a bewilderingly unwanted 'mode of locomotion' (Ch. 4). Snobbery is perhaps hardly the word for the unquestioning arrogance of these Cass men, who are used to 'parish homage,' (Ch. 9). The squire believes he has 'the hereditary duty of being noisily jovial' (Ch. 11), yet despite his self-possession and authoritativeness of voice, he is indecisive in handling his sons, following faulty indulgence with 'sudden fits of unrelentingness' (Ch. 8). In view of Godfrey's own moral weakness in not acknowledging his child when it turns up ('he had only conscience and heart enough to make him for ever uneasy under the weakness that forbade the renunciation', Ch. 13, the renunciation of Nancy Lammeter, that is), his emergence sixteen years later as squire himself, one of Silas Marner's 'better', those 'tall, powerful, florid men, seen chiefly on horseback', is highly ironic. His daughter's preference for 'working folks, and their houses, and their ways' (Ch. 19) strikes us as perfectly understandable after what we have read, quite apart from her affection for Aaron. Godfrey Cass's view of what is good for his daughter is vitiated by his sense of social superiority; he has the unjustifiable impression 'that deep affections can hardly go along with callous palms and scant means' (Ch. 17). His punishment is to fear that Eppie thinks him worse than he is; she may suspect him of having acted unjustly towards her mother (Ch. 20). But Eppie, wishing to hold to her own, is not critical of class deference as such. The 'character of Raveloe' which the New Year's Eve dance at the Red House seems to renew, confirming the social hierarchy—'what everyone had been used to' (Ch. 11)—is not to be challenged by her. The character who comes nearest to questioning the system of hereditary privilege is Aaron. When Eppie baulks at having lavender in her planned garden for the characteristic reason that lavender is to be found only in 'gentlefolks' gardens', Aaron points out that cut slips of it are just thrown away, a fact which sets him thinking about the more equal distribution of goods in society; 'there need nobody run short o' victuals if the land was made the most on, and there was never a morsel but what could find its way to a mouth' (Ch. 16). At a time when communications were so poor, such radical thought remains 'untravelled' (Ch. 1), left in the air, as it were. The possibility of organised political protest is perhaps glanced at in the sight of men and women streaming from a large factory 'for their midday meal' which meets Silas and Eppie instead of the old Lantern Yard chapel and its familiar surroundings, now 'all swept away', when they visit the northern manufacturing town years after he had left it. But the main point is still the uninformed state of rural people: we recall that 'those were not days of active inquiry and wide report' (Ch. 13). Poor communications leave Raveloe in its ravelled, tangled state.

But despite its fixed responses and hostility to strangers, the rural community *is* able to offer the disillusioned immigrant Marner a stability which is not available in the town. Significantly, he is able to exercise economic independence in Raveloe, since he is no longer working for a wholesaler-dealer. Too honest to drive 'a profitable trade in charms' and herbal remedies (Ch. 2), he accumulates wealth almost automatically and remains unpersecuted, though at first isolated. The local inability to explain his peculiarities or to suggest a context in which they could have arisen gives him a kind of negative protection, the robbery notwithstanding. When Eppie's needs furnish him with a purpose for earning, he begins to respond more positively to his human surroundings.

> —Alan W. Bellringer, *George Eliot* (New York: St. Martin's Press, 1993), pp. 75–77

PEGGY FITZHUGH JOHNSTONE ON AUTOBIOGRAPHICAL PATTERNS IN *SILAS MARNER*

[Peggy Fitzhugh Johnstone (b. 1940) is the author of *The Transformation of Rage* (1994), a study of George Eliot from which the following extract is taken. Here, Johnstone notes that many features of *Silas Marner* reflect George Eliot's own sense of grief at various calamities suffered by her own family.]

Biographic evidence, along with evidence derived from the patterns in her early fiction, suggests that through writing *Silas Marner*, Eliot was working through losses of her own. Her "intense sadness" before and during the writing of the short novel went beyond any discomfort over her "equivocal marital state," and beyond any sense of dislocation brought on by her household moves. A more serious (albeit related) matter was her estrangement from her family. Since May 1857, when she finally notified her brother Isaac of her living arrangement with Lewes, she had been a "complete outcast" from her relatives. Refusing to respond to her letter himself, Isaac had communicated his displeasure through a family lawyer; at the same time, he pressured their half-sister Fanny and their sister Chrissey to send letters breaking off all communications.

Many writers have emphasized the strength of Eliot's childhood attachment to her brother Isaac—a relationship which, as I suggested earlier, has often been compared to Maggie's with Tom in *The Mill on the Floss*. Yet judging from the references to her family in her letters, both as an adolescent and as an adult Eliot felt closer to her sister Chrissey, who had recently died, in March 1859. In letters to friends up to that point, she frequently mentions her sister, whereas references to Isaac are relatively rare.

Chrissey had been a beautiful child, and, according to Haight, her mother's favorite (along with Isaac), whereas her mother "had never been very close to Mary Anne." Nonetheless, Eliot's letters from her adolescent and young-adult years reflect her ongoing attachment to Chrissey during the period of her life when she frequently had conflicts with Isaac. When Chrissey married in May 1837, a little over a year after their mother's death, Mary Ann, as she began to spell her name at this time, became the housekeeper at Griff. Her references to Chrissey during the early years of her marriage to a struggling "medical officer" show the gradual decline of her sister's life. In her letters, Mary Ann mentions with joy the births of Chrissey's children in 1838, 1839, and 1841. Yet by June 1841, she refers to her sister's domestic life as "one continued endurance." In October she expresses sympathy for her troubles: "My dear Sister is rather an object of solicitude on many accounts—the troubles of married life seem more conspicuously the ordinance of God, in the case of one so meek and passive than in that of women who may fairly be suspected of creating half their own difficulties."

Over the years Chrissey's losses accumulated. In May 1842, her third child, only a little over a year old, died. A few years later, in February 1848, a nine-month-old baby boy died of "Hooping Cough and Convulsions." Her father, Robert Evans, died in May 1849. The following August, while Mary Ann was away recovering in Switzerland, Chrissey lost her seven-year-old daughter. Mary Ann wrote that "my heart aches to think of Chrissey with her children ill of scarlet fever—her husband almost frantic with grief and her own heart rent by the loss of this eldest little daughter." Upon her return to England, where Mary Ann reported she felt more like an "outcast" than she had in Geneva, she wrote her friend Cara Bray that "dear Chrissey is much kinder than any one else in the family and I am happiest with her. She is generous and sympathizing and really cares for my happiness."

In December 1852, Chrissey's husband died, leaving her by this time with six remaining children, "the eldest not yet fifteen years old, the youngest not fifteen months, and with little to support them" (Haight). Marian became increasingly concerned about her sister's welfare, and more than once expressed her desire to help her financially. During the following years, as Chrissey struggled to raise her children and find suitable positions for them, she lost another son, "drowned at sea," in 1855. In April 1857, she lost another daughter to typhoid fever. At that point, Eliot asked Isaac to give Chrissey fifteen pounds of her own income "to spend taking a change of air as soon as she is able to do so"; but in early May, she learned that Chrissey herself was very ill. Later that month, after she had informed her family of her life with Lewes, she wrote her friend Sara Hennell that she cared the most about staying in touch with Chrissey so that she would be able to help her, although at the time her financial capacity to help her was very limited.

In February 1859, "in the midst of . . . [the] gratifying reception of *Adam Bede,*" she finally received a letter from Chrissey, who was very ill, and who expressed regret that she had "ever ceased to write . . . one who under all circumstances was kind to me and mine." When Chrissey died shortly after, Eliot, who had already written Sara Hennell that "the past is abolished from my mind—I only want [Chrissey] to feel that I love her and care for her," wrote: "Chrissey's death has taken from the possibility of many things toward which I looked with some hope and yearning in the future. I had a very special feeling towards her, stronger than any third person would think likely."

During the years that Chrissey's life seemed to be steadily declining, Eliot was slowly finding her way to success. It seems ironic that just at the point when the publication of *Adam Bede* had established her reputation as a writer, her sister's life ended. Chrissey died on March 15, 1859, when Eliot was beginning work on *The Mill on the Floss,* and just as she was approaching the tenth anniversary of her father's death, which had occurred in May 1849. In the light of Bowlby's explanation of the way in which a recent loss, or the anniversary of a loss, or both, can activate repressed feelings of grief for an earlier one, I would argue that Eliot's sense of estrangement from her family intensified her grief (and, especially in light of her own current success, perhaps guilt) over her sister's misfortunes and death—a death which, because of its timing, revived feelings, however long repressed, associated with her parent's death. The intensity of Eliot's sadness during this period, then, could be said to derive not only from her current losses, but from the reexperiencing of unresolved feelings about past losses—the "anniversary reaction" that Pollock describes in his work on mourning. The return of Eliot's repressed feelings from the past is the "time-specific variant of the repetition-compulsion" that manifests the human mind's unconscious sense of time. Extending Marie Bonaparte's idea that the mind may associate the passing of time with death, Mintz explains that the unconscious sense of time emerging in the anniversary reaction may be crystallized out of the anxieties about death.

—Peggy Fitzhugh Johnstone, *The Transformation of Rage: Mourning and Creativity in George Eliot's Fiction* (New York: New York University Press, 1994), pp. 75–77

BERNARD SEMMEL ON SOCIAL CHANGE IN *SILAS MARNER*

[Bernard Semmel (b. 1928) is a professor of history at the State University of New York at Stony Brook. He has written *Liberalism and Naval Strategy* (1986) and *John Stuart Mill and the Pursuit of Virtue* (1984). In this extract from *George Eliot and the Politics of National Inheritance* (1994), Semmel argues that *Silas Marner* is a fable of society in a time of change.]

Silas Marner is a fable about a society in a time of change. In the traditional tale—as in the case of the heroine of *Doctor Thorne*—the princess raised as a shepherdess never hesitates to take her proper place. She is pleased to be restored to the rank to which blood assigned her, though she will no doubt reward the old shepherd who raised her so devotedly, Eppie, however, rejects the traditional code of blood in favor of a modern one of deed. She turns aside Godfrey's natural claim to her by virtue of birth in favor of Marner's earned merit as a loving father. Cass has an obligation toward Eppie, as a daughter, for whose existence he is responsible, but Eppie owes none to him merely because of blood relationship. Her moral obligation, founded upon feeling, not "lawful" right, is to Silas (chap. 19). She marries the young gardener who has long loved her, rejecting the possibility of a husband more suited to the status she might now enjoy.

George Eliot located her tale quite explicitly in the context of the social transformation from the traditional, aristocratic society to the modern one. Her first two chapters picture the traditional community of Raveloe in the last years of the Napoleonic Wars, perhaps between 1813 and 1815, when high wartime agricultural prices had made the district prosperous, and thereby supported the patriarchal predominance of the local landowners like Squire Cass. With the end of the war and the decline in agricultural prices, accompanied by continued improvements in transportation, the patriarchal authority of the landed gentry declined, and middle-class public opinion began to prevail. Godfrey and Nancy have become merely "Mr. and Mrs. Cass"—"and higher title has died away" (chap. 16). When Silas takes Eppie on a visit to the northern town from which he had journeyed some thirty years earlier, he discovers that it has become a factory town, with its former artisans replaced by an industrial proletariat. The decline of the traditional community, Eliot appears to suggest, has made possible Eppie's spirited choice of merit over blood. To employ the language of present-day social theorists, the modern criterion of "achievement" has overwhelmed the unearned feudal "ascription" of birth.

Blood itself plays an ambiguous role in this novel, as it does in other works of Eliot. Nancy's father, whose own father had come to Raveloe from somewhere in the north, is quite different in appearance from the general run of Midlands farmers. He finds this distinction "in accordance with a favorite saying of his own, that 'breed was stronger than pasture'" (chap. 11). Victorian liberals, in contrast, were apt to stress pasture over breed, environment rather than heredity. We know that the philosopher and economist John Stuart Mill and his father agreed that John Stuart's remarkable intellectual development was a product of parental education, not native ability; of achievement, not birth. This was the new society's reply to the conservative insistence, like that of the conventional romantic novel, that blood would tell. Yet the narrator pictures Eppie as startlingly different from the peasant girls of the village, for she is a lady in appearance and manner. The narrator describes Eppie's "delicate prettiness," while Silas tells her, "You're dillicate made, my dear" and notes that she needs to have somebody to work for her (chap. 16). Later, Godfrey reminds Marner that Eppie was "not fit for any hardships: she doesn't look like a strapping girl come of working parents" (chap. 19), and tells Nancy that there was not "such a pretty little girl any where else in the parish, or one fitter for the station we could give her" (chap. 17). Of course, romantic convention also played a part in Eliot's decision to portray Eppie as delicately pretty.

Silas Marner embodies an interesting departure from Eliot's championing of the modern ethos: her elevation of feeling over reason. Social theorists have written of the move from "affectivity" to "affective neutrality," the quintessentially modern effort to keep emotion in check, to strive for control. In *A Christmas Carol* Dickens had parodied through Scrooge the calculating rationality of the new middle-class society, and contrasted it with the overflowing feelings of the traditional England of the past; in *Hard Times* he contrasted the self-interested, rational bourgeois Bitzer with the loving feeling of Sissy Jupe. Similarly, in *Silas Marner,* Eppie's feelings concerning her foster father overwhelm whatever practical reasons might attract her to consider Godfrey's offer.

Despite her adoption of elements of the modern, Eliot stressed the virtues of tradition. She pictured Marner as loving "the old brick hearth as he had loved his own brown pot": "The gods of the hearth exist for us still," she declared; "and let all new faith be tolerant of that fetichism, lest it bruise its own roots." Marner tries to secure "a consciousness of unity between his past and present" (chap. 16), and Eliot made a similar effort. Eliot joined Scott and Dickens in rejecting the prosaic, commonsensical aspirations of a commercial society, with its separation of individuals from traditional communal ties. The love of Eppie replaces Marner's preoccupation with accumulation and restores him to the fellowship of *Gemeinschaft.*

The myth of the disinherited one pervades *Silas Marner,* Marner himself has been dispossessed: expelled from his sect and from his hope of salvation, he becomes a bereft wanderer, journeying with his pack from his familiar country into a strange land. Godfrey Cass lives in fear of his father's anger and rejection if his low marriage becomes known. Godfrey's long refusal to acknowledge her has disinherited Eppie. Yet when Godfrey attempts to restore to Eppie the inheritance he long denied her, she rejects his offer and yields the privileges she might enjoy because of her love for Marner, valuing the merit of both Marner and her gardener suitor. Love has led her to disinherit herself, which Eliot's philosophy of inheritance acknowledges as her right. This is the moral fable of *Silas Marner.*

—Bernard Semmel, *George Eliot and the Politics of National Inheritance* (New York: Oxford University Press, 1994), pp. 24–26

Books by
George Eliot
(Mary Ann Evans)

The Life of Jesus Critically Examined by David Friedrich Strauss (translator). 1846. 3 vols.

The Essence of Christianity by Ludwig Feuerbach (translator). 1854.

Scenes of Clerical Life. 1858. 3 vols.

Adam Bede. 1859. 3 vols.

The Mill on the Floss. 1860. 3 vols.

Silas Marner: The Weaver of Raveloe. 1861.

Romola. 1863. 2 vols.

Felix Holt, the Radical. 1866. 3 vols.

Novels. 1867–78. 6 vols.

The Spanish Gypsy. 1868.

Agatha. 1869.

How Lisa Loved the King. 1869.

Middlemarch: A Study of Provincial Life. 1872. 4 vols.

A Legend of Jubal and Other Poems. 1874.

Daniel Deronda. 1876. 4 vols.

Novels. 1876. 9 vols.

The Lifted Veil. 1878.

Works (Cabinet Edition). 1878–85. 24 vols.

Impressions of Theophrastus Such. 1879.

Essays and Leaves from a Note-Book. Ed. Charles Lee Lewes. 1884.

Poems. 1884.

George Eliot's Life as Related in Her Letters and Journals. Ed. J. W. Cross. 1885. 3 vols.

Complete Poems. 1888.

Letters to Elma Stuart 1872–1880. Ed. Roland Stuart. 1909.

Early Essays. Ed. George W. Redway. 1919.

Letters. Ed. R. Brimley Johnson. 1926.

Letters. Ed. Gordon S. Haight. 1954–78. 9 vols.

Essays. Ed. Thomas Pinney. 1963.

George Eliot's Middlemarch *Notebook: A Transcription.* Ed. John Clark Pratt and Victor A. Neufeldt. 1979.

Novels (Clarendon Edition). Ed. Gordon S. Haight. 1980– .

A Writer's Notebook 1854–1879, and Uncollected Writings. Ed. Joseph Wiesenfarth. 1981.

Ethics by Benedict Spinoza (translator). 1981.

A George Eliot Miscellany: A Supplement to Her Novels. Ed. F. B. Pinion. 1982.

Selected Critical Writings. Ed. Rosemary Ashton. 1992.

Works about George Eliot and *Silas Marner*

Barrett, Dorothea. *Vocation and Desire: George Eliot's Heroines.* London: Routledge, 1988.

Bodenheimer, Rosemarie. *The Real Life of Mary Ann Evans: George Eliot, Her Letters and Fiction.* Ithaca, NY: Cornell University Press, 1994.

Bonaparte, Felicia. "Carrying the Word of the Lord to the Gentiles: *Silas Marner* and the Translation of Scripture into a Secular Text." *Religion and Literature* 23 (1991): 39–60.

Booth, Alison. *Greatness Engendered: George Eliot and Virginia Woolf.* Ithaca, NY: Cornell University Press, 1992.

Carpenter, Mary Wilson. *George Eliot and the Language of Time: Narrative Form and Protestant Apocalyptic History.* Chapel Hill: University of North Carolina Press, 1986.

Carroll, David. *George Eliot and the Conflict of Interpretation: A Reading of the Novels.* Cambridge: Cambridge University Press, 1992.

Cottom, Daniel. *Social Figures: George Eliot, Social History and Literary Representation.* Minneapolis: University of Minnesota Press, 1987.

David, Deirdre. *Intellectual Women and Victorian Patriarchy: Harriet Martineau, Elizabeth Barrett Browning, George Eliot.* Ithaca, NY: Cornell University Press, 1987.

Dawson, Terence. " 'Light Enough to Trusten By': Structure and Experience in *Silas Marner.*" *Modern Language Review* 88 (1993): 26–45.

Dodd, Valerie A. *George Eliot: An Intellectual Life.* New York: St. Martin's Press, 1990.

Fisch, Harold. "Biblical Realism in *Silas Marner.*" In *Identity and Ethos,* ed. Mark H. Gelber. New York: Peter Lang, 1986, pp. 343–60.

Graver, Suzanne. *George Eliot and Community: A Study in Social Theory and Fictional Form.* Berkeley: University of California Press, 1984.

Handley, Graham. *George Eliot's Midlands: Passion in Exile.* London: Allison & Busby, 1991.

Karl, Frederick R. *George Eliot, Voice of a Century: A Biography.* New York: Norton, 1995.

Knoepflmacher, U. C. *George Eliot's Early Novels: The Limits of Realism.* Berkeley: University of California Press, 1968.

Mann, Karen B. *The Language That Makes George Eliot's Fiction.* Baltimore: Johns Hopkins University Press, 1983.

Martin, Carol A. *George Eliot's Serial Fiction.* Columbus: Ohio State University Press, 1994.

Nestor, Pauline. *Female Friendship and Communities: Charlotte Brontë, George Eliot, Elizabeth Gaskell.* Oxford: Clarendon Press, 1985.

Pinion, F. B. *A George Eliot Companion.* New York: Macmillan, 1981.

Prentis, Barbara. *The Brontë Sisters and George Eliot: A Unity of Difference.* Totowa, NJ: Barnes & Noble, 1987.

Spittles, Brian. *George Eliot: Godless Woman.* New York: St. Martin's Press, 1993.

Taylor, Ina. *A Woman of Contradictions: The Life of George Eliot.* New York: Morrow, 1990.

Uglow, Jennifer. *George Eliot.* New York: Pantheon, 1987.

Vitaglione, Daniel. *George Eliot and George Sand.* New York: Peter Lang, 1993.

Welsh, Alexander. *George Eliot and Blackmail.* Cambridge, MA: Harvard University Press, 1985.

Index of
Themes and Ideas